NC

NARROW CANYON PUBLISHING

UNSTUCK
EMAIL

EMAIL ISN'T DEAD

YOU'RE JUST DOING IT WRONG

JOHN ELDER

NARROW CANYON PUBLISHING

New York London Toronto Sydney Singapore

FOR APRIL
As Always

Other Books By John Elder

CODING BOOKS

Intro To Python Programming:
Beginners Guide Series

Intro To Python Programming:
Beginners Guide Series Workbook

Intro To Ruby Programming:
Beginners Guide Series

Learn Ruby On Rails For Web Development

Tkinter Widget Quick Reference Guide

PHP Programming For Affiliate Marketers

MARKETING BOOKS

The Smart Startup:
How To Crush It Without Falling Into The Venture Capital Trap

Living The Dot Com Lifestyle:
The Ultimate Guide To Independence and Financial Glory

Adsense Niche Sites Unleashed

Table of Contents

Table of Contents (continued)

UNSTUCK
EMAIL

INTRODUCTION

If You're Sick of Emails Failing and Bosses Blaming You, This Might Be the Book That Finally Changes Everything...

Let me guess. You're staring at your email dashboard again. Your open rates are flat. Click-throughs? Embarrassing. Replies? Nowhere to be found.

Your boss just sent you yet another message about "maybe trying LinkedIn Ads instead."

And honestly, you want to scream.

But instead, you sip a cold cup of coffee, open Google, and type the same phrase you've searched too many times already:

"Why did my email go to spam Gmail?"

And somewhere deep down, you start wondering if the problem... might be you.

It's not.

I know because I've been exactly where you are. And this book? I wrote it for you.

This Isn't Just About Email. It's About Control.

When email works, it feels effortless. You send a message. People open. They click. Some even buy. Your metrics go up. Your boss nods in approval. You feel like a pro.

But when email doesn't work? It's invisible.

Your work gets buried. Your confidence slips. You wonder if anyone even saw your message—let alone cared.

That's not just a marketing problem. That's a meaning problem. Because let's be honest... it hurts when your best work vanishes.

It makes you second-guess everything. Am I even good at this? Is email just dead now? Why does everyone else seem to be winning?

I've asked those questions, too.

Until I met someone who made me want to answer them for real. Her name was Jenna.

Meet Jenna: The Underdog Email Marketer With a Swipe File and a Secret

Jenna isn't new to this game. She's written onboarding flows, launched SaaS products, A/B tested weird subject lines, and devoured more copywriting podcasts than most people know exist.

She's smart. Scrappy. Sharp. But something changed. What used to work... didn't. Her metrics tanked. Her CEO questioned her strategy. And her inbox? It stopped delivering.

One Monday morning, she sent a campaign to her 9,000-person list. The open rate was 11.2 percent. Click-through? 0.3 percent. Replies? Zero.

She stared at her dashboard. Then she stared at the Slack message from her boss:

"Should we just try LinkedIn Ads instead?"

She didn't respond. Not because she didn't care. Because she didn't have a defense. At least, not yet.

This Book Is That Defense. But More Than That, It's a Plan.

You're not holding another theory book. You're not about to read 200 pages of fluff or get lectured by a guru with a personal brand and a ring light. You're about to get a roadmap.

This is the exact process Jenna used to go from discouraged and doubtful...to running email campaigns that outperformed paid ads, won internal trust, and actually got people talking again.

She didn't add fancy designs. She didn't chase new platforms. She didn't "hack" deliverability. She learned how email really works—and rebuilt from the ground up. And now, you're about to do the same.

"Spam Filters Aren't Killing Your Emails. Bad Strategy Is."

You've probably been told...Use a catchy subject line. Try emojis. Send Tuesdays at 10am. Make your emails look amazing.

But here's what they didn't tell you...If your domain's not authenticated, it doesn't matter how clever your copy is. If your list is bloated with dead weight, Gmail will bury you. If no one ever replies to your emails, inboxes stop trusting you. That's the truth.

And this book? It gives you the tools, language, and tactics to fix it. Even if you've never touched a DNS record. Even if you think "DMARC" sounds like a rapper. Even if you've been burned by promises before.

Here's What You'll Learn (Even If You Don't Speak Tech)

By the time you finish this book, you'll know how to:

- Fix your sender reputation and finally get seen
- Design emails that look like personal notes, not promotions
- Prune your list without fear—and watch your metrics climb
- Ask for replies in ways that actually get them
- Spot the metrics that matter (and ignore the ones that lie)
- Earn trust, build engagement, and finally stop guessing

You'll also know how to explain this stuff to your boss. So the next time someone asks if email's still worth it? You won't blink. You'll have data. You'll have clarity. You'll have control.

This Book Works Best for a Certain Kind of Person.

It's not for people chasing shiny tactics. It's not for marketers who want to blast 10,000 strangers and cross their fingers. It's not for gurus who think growth equals shouting louder.

It's for you. The builder. The fixer. The one who still believes email can work—but needs proof. The person who's tired of "best practices" that don't apply. The marketer who wants to be heard without being salesy.

Respected without being flashy. Successful without being loud. If that sounds like you? Keep reading.

Email Isn't Dying. It's Growing Up.

People say email's dead. They're wrong. What's dead is lazy email. What's dead is the idea that you can spray and pray and win.

What's alive is email that feels like a real person wrote it. Email that lands in inboxes. Email that gets replies. Email that builds trust.

The old rules are gone. The game has changed. And this book gives you the new playbook.

You're Not Broken. The System Is Rigged. Here's How to Beat It.

You're not bad at email. You're just playing with old tools in a new world. This book gives you the right tools. It gives you real steps. Real proof. Real freedom.

You don't need to be louder. You don't need to be trendier. You don't need to be anyone but yourself—smart, curious, capable, and ready. What you need now… is a win.

So turn the page. Because that win is waiting.

— John Elder
Spamnesty.com

Chapter 1
The Big Lie:
Email Is Dying

Section 1: Why Everyone Thinks Email Is Dead

(And Why They're Wrong)

"The reports of my death are greatly exaggerated."
— Mark Twain

J enna Blake wasn't new to email marketing. She'd been running campaigns for over seven years, starting back when open rates were easy wins and click-throughs came with just the right subject line. She'd built nurture sequences, launched SaaS products, run onboarding flows, and written dozens of newsletters. And for a long time, that was enough. The numbers came in, the charts pointed upward, and the CEO nodded in approval.

But this time, everything was different.

It was a Monday morning, and Jenna was sitting at her kitchen counter, laptop open, half-drunk cup of coffee to her left. Her dashboard stared back at her. She refreshed it once. Twice. No change. Her open rate for the latest campaign had flatlined at 11.2%. Click-through? 0.3%. One spam complaint. Three unsubscribes. Zero replies. Her list size? Just over 9,000. Her self-confidence? Dropping like a rock.

She closed the browser tab, opened Slack, and stared at a message from her boss:

"Just read this. Should we think about moving budget to LinkedIn Ads?"

Attached was a link to a blog post titled: "Is Email Still Worth It in 2025?"

Jenna didn't respond. She didn't have a defense. At least, not yet.

The Beginning of the Blame Game

When email campaigns flop, most marketers go through the same mental checklist:
- Was the subject line strong enough?
- Was the timing right?
- Should we have used emojis?
- Was the design too busy? Too plain?

And if nothing obvious stands out, they do what everyone eventually does: they blame the spam filter. Or Gmail. Or the algorithm. Or the consumer. Or Apple's Mail Privacy Protection.

Or Gen Z. Or AI-generated content. Or the fact that nobody reads anymore.

Because blaming the system is easier than questioning your approach.

This is the lie we've told ourselves. The one that spreads in webinars, in Slack threads, in Twitter arguments and LinkedIn comments. The one that whispers: "It's not you. It's email. Email is just… over."

But email isn't over. Email is evolving. And most marketers never evolved with it.

The Persistence of a Convenient Myth

It's comforting to believe that email is dying. If the system is broken, you're not responsible for the results. If no one reads email anymore, then it doesn't matter how good your copy was. If Gmail is too strict, then it's not your fault your messages went to spam. If open rates are declining across the board, then your 9% is just the new normal.

These explanations feel good—until you look at the numbers.

Because while some marketers are fighting to break 15% open rates, others are quietly earning 30%, 40%, even 50%. While some are seeing revenue dry up, others are building multi-million-dollar businesses entirely from email. And while some scream about the death of email, others are doubling down and building defensible, direct-response engines that outperform any social or paid ad campaign.

So what gives?

The Real Problem Isn't Email. It's Misuse.

Let's be blunt: most marketers don't understand email. Not really. They understand headlines, A/B testing, maybe copywriting. But they don't understand the infrastructure. They don't understand sender reputation. They don't understand deliverability mechanics, spam

21

score thresholds, or the behavioral algorithms that sort email long before a human sees it.

And the advice they've followed for years? Much of it is outdated, diluted, or just plain wrong.

They were told to design beautiful HTML emails. They were told to send at 10am on Tuesdays. They were told to focus on subject lines. They were told to automate everything. They were told to grow the list at any cost. They were told unsubscribes were bad. They were told re-engagement campaigns were best practice.

And slowly, quietly, these ideas turned email marketing into a bloated, over-optimized, under-performing machine. A machine that no longer earned attention—but demanded it. That no longer felt personal, but promotional. That stopped being a conversation, and started being a broadcast.

And people tuned out.

But email didn't die. It just got worse. And those who learned how to do it right are reaping the rewards.

Why Email Still Wins

Here's what hasn't changed: email is the only channel that gives you direct, algorithm-free access to your audience. No boosting. No bidding. No dancing for engagement. When someone gives you their email address, they're giving you permission to speak directly to them —on their time, in their space, without interference.

You own the list. You control the send. You can track engagement, reply behavior, and sales. You can move platforms. You can export your data. You can build workflows, automations, sequences, campaigns, newsletters—and they all belong to you.

That's power. And most marketers have forgotten how rare that power is.

Because they're too distracted chasing impressions on platforms that don't belong to them. Platforms that can shut off their reach with a change in policy or an algorithm tweak. Platforms that make them pay to access the audience they already built.

Email doesn't do that.

But it does require you to play by rules. And most marketers are playing the wrong game.

Deliverability Is Not a Mystery

One of the biggest lies in email marketing is that spam filters are random. That they're black boxes. That no one really knows how they work. That you can do everything right and still get punished.

Wrong.

Spam filters are not random. They are rule-based systems that rely on behavioral signals to evaluate your trustworthiness as a sender. They look at whether people open your emails, click links, reply, forward, archive, delete without opening, or mark as spam.

They look at your bounce rate, your unsubscribe rate, your complaint rate. They look at whether your sending domain is authenticated with SPF, DKIM, and DMARC. They look at your sending patterns, your IP reputation, and how your recent campaigns performed.

All of this adds up to a sender reputation. And that reputation is what determines whether your email lands in the inbox, the promotions tab, or the spam folder.

It's not magic. It's mechanics. And you can control it.

But only if you understand it.

What Jenna Discovered

After that campaign tanked, Jenna did what most don't: she investigated. She opened up Google Postmaster Tools. She ran her domain through MXToolbox. She read about SPF, DKIM, and DMARC—and realized her domain was only partially authenticated. She looked at her HTML code and saw image-to-text ratios that flagged every best practice guide. She realized she hadn't cleaned her list in over a year.

So she changed everything.

She stripped out the design. She rewrote her emails in plain, personal language. She segmented her list by recent engagement. She deleted 2,000 subscribers who hadn't opened in 90 days. She started sending from a subdomain and warming it slowly. She added a simple P.S. asking people to reply if they wanted the next resource.

Her next send went to 7,000 people. Open rate: 27%. Click-through: 3.1%. Four replies. Zero spam complaints.

And for the first time in six months, she felt like email worked again.

Because it did.

Why This Book Exists

This book is not about theory. It's not about trends. It's not about "the future of marketing" or speculative predictions.

It's about what works right now. It's about how to rebuild email marketing from the ground up—based on real rules, not recycled advice.

It's about understanding:

- How spam filters actually work

- How to fix your infrastructure

- How to design emails that look personal

- How to build reputation from scratch

- How to measure what matters

- How to write for the inbox, not just the eye

- How to earn replies, clicks, and trust

And above all, it's about rejecting the idea that email is dead.

Because it's not.

It's just waiting for smart marketers to treat it with the respect it deserves.

Up Next: The Rules They Don't Teach You

In the next section, we'll go deep into the mechanics of email infrastructure and sender reputation. We'll break down the technical barriers that scare most marketers away—and show you how to set up a bulletproof foundation for inbox success.

Because once you stop guessing, you start winning.

Chapter 1 - Section 2

What Really Determines Whether You Land in the Inbox

When Jenna first heard terms like SPF, DKIM, or DMARC, her eyes glazed over. They sounded like technical jargon meant for IT teams, not marketers. But what she would soon learn—and what most marketers still don't understand—is that those acronyms form the backbone of your email's deliverability.

Email, unlike most modern communication channels, operates on a 40-year-old infrastructure. It's built on protocols, not platforms. That means your emails aren't subject to some opaque, centralized moderation like social media posts. Instead, inbox providers like Gmail, Yahoo, and Outlook evaluate every message based on a mix of sender reputation, engagement metrics, and authentication protocols.

Understanding how those systems work isn't optional anymore. It's the difference between inbox placement and total invisibility.

The Three Pillars of Trust: SPF, DKIM, and DMARC

Let's break it down simply:

• SPF (Sender Policy Framework) tells inbox providers which servers are allowed to send email on your behalf. Without SPF, a spammer could spoof your email address.

• DKIM (DomainKeys Identified Mail) uses a digital signature to verify that your email hasn't been altered in transit. It proves that the content of your message came from your domain and hasn't been tampered with.

• DMARC (Domain-based Message Authentication, Reporting & Conformance) builds on SPF and DKIM. It tells inbox providers what to do if an email fails those checks—whether to reject it, quarantine it, or let it through. It also gives you reports on what's being sent from your domain.

Set up correctly, these three protocols act like a verified badge for your domain. They tell the email world: this sender is legit.

If they're missing or misconfigured, however, you're sending with a red flag attached to every message.

Reputation is Everything

Your sender reputation is like a credit score for your domain and IP address. And just like a credit score, it's invisible to you unless you check.

It's shaped by factors like:

- Bounce rates

- Spam complaints

- Open rates

- Reply rates

- Click-through rates

- List hygiene

- Sending consistency

Jenna learned this the hard way. After a year of inconsistent campaigns, sporadic list cleaning, and poor infrastructure, her domain had developed a weak reputation. Every time she hit "send," Gmail rolled its eyes.

Reputation takes time to build, and only a few bad decisions to tank.

How to Check Your Reputation

Thankfully, tools exist:

• **Google Postmaster Tools**: If you send more than a few thousand emails per day, Google Postmaster gives you insights into your domain's performance inside Gmail.

• **MxToolbox**: A quick diagnostic tool for seeing if your domain appears on any blacklists.

• **Talos Intelligence** (from Cisco): Shows IP and domain reputation data.

• **Senderscore.org**: Provides a 0–100 score based on your IP reputation (higher is better).

If your scores are low, inboxes will punish you, no matter how good your content is. If your scores are high, you have the technical greenlight—and your fate is left to engagement.

The Engagement Equation

Inbox providers track behavior like hawks. Every time a recipient:

• Opens your email

• Clicks a link

• Replies

• Forwards it

• Moves it to another folder

• Saves it

• Marks it as "not spam"

They're telling the algorithm: "This sender matters."

On the flip side, when people:

• Delete without reading

• Leave unopened

• Let emails pile up unread

• Mark as spam

• Unsubscribe at high rates

...you lose trust.

What matters most isn't your clickbait headline. It's how your audience behaves over time.

List Hygiene: Quality Over Quantity

Jenna had 9,000 subscribers on her list. She was proud of that number. But only 3,000 had opened in the last 90 days. A full 2,500 hadn't opened anything in over a year.

That dead weight wasn't harmless. It was quietly dragging her engagement metrics down, making her look like a spammer.

Once she deleted those cold subs, her engagement rates jumped. And Gmail noticed.

Many marketers fear cutting their list. They think size equals strength. But the opposite is true in deliverability. Smaller, more engaged lists perform better. They inbox more reliably. They build reputation faster. They generate more revenue per send.

The Cost of Ignorance

Marketers who ignore infrastructure are like chefs who ignore the oven.

They focus on the ingredients. The recipe. The plating. But if the oven doesn't heat properly, the dish will fail.

In email, your infrastructure is the oven. If your SPF is broken, if your domain is untrusted, if your engagement is weak, your emails will fail—no matter how brilliant your copy is.

It's not fair. But it is consistent.

Design Is a Signal, Not Just a Style

HTML-heavy emails with multiple columns, buttons, and images often look amazing to marketers.

To spam filters, they look like promotional offers.

The more an email looks like a brand blast, the more likely it gets routed to the Promotions tab or filtered outright.

Plain-text or lightly formatted emails tend to inbox better. They feel personal. They look like they came from a human being, not a corporate server.

This doesn't mean all design is bad. But it does mean design has consequences. And if you're struggling to inbox, stripping out your visuals is often the fastest fix.

Reply Rates: The Ultimate Inbox Signal

Gmail loves replies. They indicate two-way conversation, relevance, and trust.

Marketers often think about opens and clicks. But replies are far more powerful. They signal real human engagement.

Jenna started adding CTAs like:

• "Reply with YES if you want next week's strategy."

• "Hit reply and tell me what's not working for you."

It wasn't just about gathering insights. It was about earning trust - from both her audience and the inbox.

Her reply rate went from near zero to 4.6%. And her inbox rate followed.

The Myth of the Re-engagement Campaign

You've probably heard this before:

"Before deleting cold subs, run a re-engagement campaign. Give them one last chance."

The logic sounds fair. But in practice, it often backfires. Re-engagement campaigns tend to have:

• Low open rates

• Low click-through

• High spam complaints

And they tank your metrics right when you need a rebound. Jenna skipped hers. She didn't ask dead subscribers for permission to stay. She just removed them. Quietly. Respectfully. Permanently.

And her results improved almost instantly.

Consistency Builds Trust

Gmail doesn't just track what you send. It tracks when you send.

Erratic sending patterns—like blasting 30,000 emails in a day, then disappearing for a couple months—raise red flags. Consistent rhythms build trust. Weekly. Biweekly. Even monthly. Pick a cadence and stick to it.

Also, warming up matters. New domains need time to build trust. Start small, gradually increasing volume. Don't go from zero to 10,000 in a week. That's how spammers operate. And Gmail knows it.

Smart Sending Starts Here

By fixing her infrastructure, pruning her list, and refocusing on real engagement, Jenna completely changed her trajectory. Her next campaign landed a 35.7% open rate, a 4.9% click-through, and zero spam complaints.

Email started working again. Not because the content changed— but because the foundation did.

This is what most marketers miss. They obsess over what's inside the email, and ignore everything around it. They blame the inbox when they should be inspecting their setup.

Email is a technical channel. But it rewards human connection. The better you understand the system, the more room you have to express your message.

In the next section, we'll dive into what it really means to write for the inbox. Because once you've built the infrastructure, the next step is clarity, tone, timing, and the psychology of engagement.

The tech gets you through the door. The writing earns you the welcome.

Chapter 1 - Section 3

The New Rules of Email and the Rise of Quiet Rebels

The people who say email is dying aren't entirely wrong—they're just looking at the wrong inbox. If you measure success by vanity metrics, by flashy design, by big sends and quick bursts of activity, then yes, email may appear dead. But if you measure success by connection, consistency, and actual outcomes - appointments booked, revenue generated, loyalty earned —email is not only alive, it's more powerful than ever.

The reason is simple: inboxes are getting smarter, and so are the marketers who respect them.

The Counterculture of Email Marketing

There is a quiet revolution happening.

A group of marketers—copywriters, strategists, founders, and operators—have stopped trying to game the system. They don't chase trends. They don't obsess over emojis or dayparting. They build real engagement, one email at a time.

These marketers understand that email is no longer about volume. It's about velocity through the funnel. It's about targeting segments instead of blasting lists. It's about reply rates instead of open rates. It's about building reputation, not just reach.

And it's working.

These quiet rebels are getting 30% open rates. 50% reply rates on onboarding sequences. 20%+ click-throughs on emails that look like they were sent from a friend. They're writing in lowercase subject lines. They're ditching buttons. They're pruning their lists every month. They're using Google Postmaster Tools like marketers use Google Analytics.

They're not loud. But they're winning.

The New Rules of the Inbox

Let's break down the new laws governing successful email marketing.

1. Simpler Emails Win

Plain-text or light-HTML emails feel personal. They land better. They read faster. They work. Jenna learned this the moment she dropped her fancy template and sent a message that sounded like a Slack DM.

2. The Best CTA is a Reply

Not a button. Not a link. A reply. Why? Because replies tell inbox providers your email matters. They build trust. They build rapport. They start conversations.

Ask real questions. Use binary CTAs. Prompt action like:

- "Want the case study? Reply YES."

- "Want me to shut up? Reply NO."

- "Quick poll—Reply 1, 2, or 3."

3. Less Is More

Every word you add to an email is a reason for someone to stop reading. Tight emails win. Short paragraphs win. Skimmable formatting wins.

Structure your email like this:

- Hook

- 1-2 punchy paragraphs

- CTA

- P.S.

That's it.

4. Earn the Right to Be Long

There's a time for long emails—but only after trust is built. Don't start with 1,500 words. Start with 150 that hit. Then expand.

5. Subject Lines Don't Have to Sell

They just need to be interesting. Subject lines that look like internal memos get opened:

- "quick update"

- "draft attached"

- "got 5 mins?"

That doesn't mean trick people. It means blend into their day.

6. Schedule is a Signal

Inboxes crave consistency. Sending every Tuesday at 10AM isn't magic —but being consistent is. Gmail tracks patterns. So pick a rhythm and stick to it.

7. Prune Without Permission

Don't ask cold subs if they still want to hear from you. Remove them. Protect your reputation.

8. Stop Sending to Everyone

Segmentation is everything. If someone only clicked on product A, don't send them product B. Respect what people told you with their behavior.

9. Write Like a Human

Jargon kills interest. Formality kills connection. Write how you talk. If you wouldn't say it to a friend over coffee, don't write it.

10. Respect the Inbox

Email isn't a billboard. It's a handshake. Treat every send like a favor you're asking. Because it is.

Jenna's New Playbook

By the end of her first quarter rebuilding email from the ground up, Jenna had transformed not just her metrics, but her reputation inside the company. Her emails were generating demo requests. Partners were replying. Her CEO asked her to train the sales team.

Her old campaigns felt like shouting into the void. Her new ones? They felt like conversations.

The list was smaller, but it was stronger. The open rates were higher. But more importantly, the outcomes were real.

Because she stopped believing the lie. And started learning the rules.

From Broadcast to Conversation

The biggest mindset shift for Jenna wasn't technical. It was emotional. She stopped thinking of email as a campaign. And started thinking of it as a relationship.

Broadcast thinking says:

- "We have to tell everyone."

- "We need a big splash."

- "More people equals more power."

Relationship thinking says:

- "Who wants this right now?"

- "What's the simplest way to help?"

- "How can I earn the next reply?"

And that shift changed everything.

You Don't Need to Be Loud. You Need to Be Clear.

You don't need to be clever. You don't need to be flashy. You don't need to win awards.

You need to show up, consistently, with clarity, humility, and something worth saying.

The inbox rewards that. The market rewards that. The reader—Jenna, or someone like her—rewards that.

Because she's not looking for another marketing campaign. She's looking for someone who understands.

Section Recap: Email Isn't Dying—Bad Email Is

To wrap up, let's remember what we've learned:

- Email still has the best ROI of any digital channel.

- Inbox placement is driven by behavior, not luck.

- Infrastructure matters. Reputation matters. Replies matter.

- Smaller, cleaner lists beat large, disengaged ones.

- Simpler formatting works better.

- Clear, personal writing outperforms hype.

- Consistency and trust are the long game.

Email didn't die. It matured. Now, it rewards the people who respect it.

In the next chapter, we'll explore sender reputation in detail—why it's your new subject line, and how to build it from the ground up.

Because if you want to land in the inbox, you don't need more hype. You need more trust.

Chapter 2

Signal Boosters:

Reputation Is The New Subject Line

Section 1: Why Your Reputation Matters

More Than Your Copy

"It takes 20 years to build a reputation and five minutes to ruin it."
— Warren Buffett

A sk any struggling email marketer what they're focused on, and you'll hear the same answers: subject lines, open rates, click-throughs, maybe a little segmentation. But ask a high-performing sender what they focus on, and you'll hear something entirely different: reputation.

Your sender reputation is the single biggest factor in determining whether your emails get seen at all. It controls whether Gmail trusts you. It shapes how Outlook treats you. It decides whether your next message goes to the inbox, the promotions tab, or straight to spam.

And the irony? Most marketers don't even know they have one.

The Truth Behind Deliverability

Subject lines might get you the open. Copy might get the click. But neither matter if your email never lands in the inbox to begin with.

Inbox placement is determined by a combination of:

• Technical setup (SPF, DKIM, DMARC)

• Domain and IP reputation

• List hygiene and engagement

• Sending consistency

• Behavioral signals from recipients (opens, clicks, replies, deletes, complaints)

This ecosystem is always in motion. Every send affects your future sends. Every recipient action is a vote for or against your trustworthiness. You are constantly earning or losing favor with every campaign.

And subject lines? They only matter after all that.

Reputation is Like a Credit Score

Imagine applying for a mortgage. You have a great personality. You say all the right things. But your credit score is 460.

It doesn't matter what you say. You're not getting the loan.

That's how inboxes treat your domain and IP. They score you based on your history:

• Do you send to people who actually engage?

• Do you clean your list?

• Do people reply or delete your emails without opening them?

• Do you send from authenticated domains?

• Do you send consistently or sporadically?

The higher your score, the more inboxes trust you. The lower your score, the more they ignore you.

And unlike subject lines or design, reputation can't be fixed overnight.

Gmail: The Gatekeeper

Gmail handles more than 1.8 billion active inboxes. If you're sending to consumers, founders, indie professionals, or even corporate teams using Google Workspace, you're probably landing in Gmail.

Gmail is also the strictest gatekeeper. Their algorithm doesn't just scan your content. It watches your behavior over time.

• Sudden spikes in volume? Red flag.

• Low engagement over 60 days? Red flag.

- Too many promotional elements? Promotions tab.

- Unusual complaint rate? Spam folder.

If you want to win with email, you have to win with Gmail.
That starts with reputation.

Why Marketers Ignore This

Marketers are trained to think about campaigns. Design. Copy. Offers. Headlines.

But reputation isn't visual. It doesn't show up in a split test. You can't A/B test it easily. It requires patience, discipline, and a systems mindset.

Which is why most marketers ignore it—until it's too late.

Jenna's Wake-Up Call

Jenna had been chasing subject lines. She ran experiments every week: brackets, emojis, urgency, curiosity gaps. She had a whole Notion board of tested phrases.

And her open rates still tanked.

It wasn't until she ran a domain health check that she realized the issue wasn't her copy. It was her sender score. Her domain had taken too many hits: high bounce rates, infrequent sends, stale list segments.

So she started over.

She built a sending plan that warmed her IP slowly. She set up SPF, DKIM, and DMARC correctly. She deleted cold subscribers instead of "re-engaging" them. She segmented by recent activity only.

And her reputation improved.

That's when her emails started getting opened again.

A New Paradigm: Reputation First

In the old world of email, everything started with the message

Today, everything starts with the sender.

Inbox providers aren't reading your email like a human. They're evaluating you like a database entry. Your metrics shape your fate.

This means you have to earn the right to be read.

Before you worry about what to say, worry about whether you'll be heard at all.

In the next section, we'll break down exactly how to measure, manage, and improve your reputation—using tools most marketers don't even know exist.

Because if you can master reputation, everything else gets easier.

Chapter 2 - Section 2

Building, Monitoring, and Repairing Your Reputation

When Jenna realized her sender reputation was the root of her deliverability issues, her first reaction was overwhelm. Where do you even begin fixing something invisible? Reputation isn't listed in your ESP dashboard. Gmail doesn't send you warnings. There's no alarm that goes off when your domain starts sinking.

And yet, almost everything in your email strategy flows from it.

Luckily, sender reputation isn't magic. It's just misunderstood.

Let's pull back the curtain on how to monitor, build, and repair your reputation—starting with the tools that give you visibility.

Essential Tools for Monitoring Sender Reputation

Most marketers never use these tools. That alone gives you a huge edge.

Google Postmaster Tools

• If you send to Gmail addresses at scale, this is your window into how Google sees you.

• You'll see metrics like domain reputation (High, Medium, Low, Bad), spam complaint rates, authentication status, and delivery errors.

• To use it, you'll need to verify ownership of your domain.

MxToolbox

• Great for checking blacklist status, SPF/DKIM setup, and general domain health.

• Also shows DNS errors and mail server configuration problems.

Sender Score (by Validity)

• Rates your IP on a 0–100 scale based on global data.

• A score below 80 means inboxing issues are likely.

Cisco Talos Intelligence

• Offers real-time IP and domain reputation data from a security standpoint.

• Helps you understand how your sending domain is seen across different threat databases.

Mail-Tester.com

• Send an email to the address they provide, and get a full breakdown of deliverability factors.

• Useful for previewing how spammy your message appears.

Jenna began using Postmaster Tools weekly. She tracked her reputation trend like a stock ticker. Within a month, her domain reputation rose from "Low" to "Medium." By the second month, she hit "High." And her inbox placement followed suit.

Authentication: The Cost of Neglect

If you're sending unauthenticated email, you might as well be wearing a ski mask to a job interview.

Authentication tells inbox providers that your email really came from you. It's a basic trust signal. Without it, even engaged subscribers might never see your message.

Here's how each one works:

• **SPF**: A DNS record that lists which mail servers are allowed to send on your behalf.

• **DKIM**: Digitally signs your message with a private key. The receiving server checks it against your public key.

• **DMARC**: Tells receiving servers what to do if SPF or DKIM fail—and sends reports back to you.

Together, these form the "trust triangle" of email authentication.

It's not enough to set these up once. You need to verify them regularly. Tools like DMARC Analyzer can help you parse the XML reports DMARC sends, which are unreadable by default.

Warming Up a Cold Domain

If you're launching a new domain, or reviving one that's been dormant, you need to warm it up.

Here's a simplified sequence:

• **Week 1**: Send to 50 engaged subscribers. Keep messages simple, personal, and ask for replies.

• **Week 2**: Double the volume. Keep engagement high.

• **Week 3-4**: Continue scaling while maintaining a 20-30% open rate and low bounce/complaint rates.

• **Week 5+**: Once you hit 1,000+ daily sends, you can begin regular campaign volume.

The key is engagement. If your early emails are ignored or flagged, your domain reputation will crater before you even begin.

List Hygiene as a Trust Mechanism

Your list is not a trophy. It's a liability if unmanaged.

Jenna had been holding onto a list of over 9,000 contacts. But only a fraction had engaged in the last 60 days. Her unsubscribe rate was creeping up. So was her complaint rate.

She built a 3-tiered system:

Tier 1: Engaged in the last 30 days

- Receives full campaigns

- Eligible for replies, case studies, direct offers

Tier 2: Engaged in last 31-90 days

- Receives lighter content

- Focus on value, warming back up

Tier 3: No engagement in 90+ days

- Suppressed or removed silently

This cleaned version of her list got 42% higher open rates and fewer complaints almost immediately.

How Replies Build Reputation

Gmail's algorithm prioritizes human engagement. And nothing says "this message matters" like a reply.

Encourage replies by:

- Asking binary questions

- Using first-person, plain tone

- Avoiding no-reply email addresses

- Promising a response (and delivering)

Sample CTAs:

- "Reply and I'll send the doc."

- "What's your biggest challenge?"

- "Want this? Just reply yes."

Every reply is a vote for your reputation.

Sending Cadence: Don't Be a Stranger

Inconsistent sending is one of the most common reputation killers.

If you go dark for weeks, then blast your list with a campaign, you look like a spammer.

Pick a cadence:

- Weekly

- Bi-weekly

- Monthly (minimum)

Stick to it. The algorithm likes rhythm. So do readers.

Fixing a Damaged Reputation

What if you've already taken a hit?

Step 1: Pause all sends for 48-72 hours

Step 2: Authenticate everything. Recheck SPF, DKIM, DMARC.

Step 3: Build a "health list" of your most engaged subscribers (last 14 days).

Step 4: Resume sending only to that segment. Ask for replies. Measure metrics.

Step 5: Slowly add more segments over 2-4 weeks, watching bounce and complaint rates.

Step 6: Monitor with Postmaster Tools, MxToolbox, and Sender Score.

Step 7: Repeat the pattern until metrics stabilize.

Repairing reputation is possible—but it requires discipline.

Reputation Is a Living System

It's not a switch you flip. It's a system you maintain.

Reputation is shaped by everything you do:

• How clean your list is

• How often you send

• How people engage

• Whether you reply to replies

• How your infrastructure is configured

Every email is a signal. Every signal is a vote. Every vote adds up.

Jenna's journey wasn't a one-time fix. It became a process:

• Weekly list hygiene

• Monthly authentication checks

• Quarterly infrastructure audits

• Real-time monitoring of engagement metrics

She built systems. And the systems protected her sender status.

In the next section, we'll dig into how to use reputation proactively—not just to avoid spam, but to earn placement, attention, and trust at scale.

Because reputation isn't just a defensive shield. It's your competitive advantage.

Chapter 2 - Section 3

Engineering a Reputation Driven Strategy

If sender reputation is the foundation of inbox success, then it needs to be baked into your strategy from the beginning—not slapped on as a bandage when things go wrong. The best email marketers don't just react to reputation problems. They engineer their entire strategy around maintaining and boosting reputation over time.

This means aligning your content, cadence, segmentation, and analytics to signal trust continuously.

Proactive Reputation Management

You don't need a reputation recovery plan if you never fall in the first place. Jenna learned this after spending months repairing her domain's standing. Once she stabilized, she made reputation a part of her planning process.

She treated it like hygiene. Not an emergency. A daily habit.

That meant every new campaign followed a checklist:

• Are we sending to the most engaged audience?

• Is our list fully cleaned and verified?

• Are we maintaining our sending rhythm?

• Is this message designed to generate engagement?

• Have we tested the technical side with Mail-Tester or a seed list?

Jenna also built alerts using Google Sheets and Postmaster Tools. If her spam complaint rate exceeded 0.2% or her open rate dipped below 15%, she got a Slack notification.

Small moves. Big protection.

Segmenting for Signal

Reputation isn't just about the size of your audience. It's about how that audience behaves.

Instead of one big list, Jenna created segments based on engagement recency:

- Hot (0-30 days engaged)

- Warm (31-60 days)

- Cool (61-90 days)

- Cold (91+ days)

Only Hot and Warm segments received campaigns with direct offers or reply CTAs. Cool segments received content-only emails to try and revive them. Cold contacts were silently pruned.

This kept her engagement rate high, which in turn kept her reputation high.

Designing for Deliverability

Email design isn't just aesthetic. It's reputational.

Every time you:

- Add an image

- Use bold formatting

- Include a button

- Drop in custom fonts or multiple links

...you're sending subtle signals to spam filters.

Does that mean you should never use these elements? No. But you must test.

Jenna ran A/B tests where the only difference was design:

• Plain-text vs HTML

• Button vs hyperlinked text

• One-column vs multi-column

In nearly every case, the simpler design outperformed—not in clicks, but in inbox placement.

She started using light HTML emails: basic branding, inline CSS, single column, text-based CTA.

No spam trigger words. No images above the fold. No more than three links per message.

Using Engagement Pods Intelligently

You may have heard of engagement pods—small groups of people who open and reply to each other's emails to boost reputation.

When done wrong, they're spammy and transparent. When done right, they can be effective.

Jenna built an internal engagement list: ten team members, partners, and friendly vendors. Every campaign went to them first. Their job?

• Open it quickly

• Reply

• Mark it as important

• Forward to a colleague

These signals gave the email momentum before it hit the rest of the list.

Think of it like sending up a signal flare. Gmail noticed. And rewarded the message.

Gamifying Replies

To make replies easier, Jenna embedded mini-games into her messages:

• "Reply YES, NO, or MAYBE"

• "Choose A, B, or C"

• "If you're curious, just reply with the word INSIGHT"

This turned replies from a task into a game.

She also set up automatic thank-you responses for anyone who replied. These weren't just transactional. They made people feel heard.

Example:

"Got your message. Thanks for engaging—it really helps with inboxing. You'll get something great next week."

Building a Reply Culture

One of the best-kept secrets in email marketing is reply culture. When you train your audience to expect personal responses, they engage more.

Jenna started replying to every 10th email manually. She asked follow-ups. She shared resources. She made jokes.

Her readers noticed. They started replying more.

And that loop reinforced her reputation.

Using Pre-Send Metrics

Before sending a campaign, Jenna checked:

- Engagement health of the list

- Spam score from Mail-Tester

- Inbox placement via GlockApps (seed list test)

If anything looked off, she paused the send. Better to delay than damage reputation.

Time-of-Day Testing for ISP Behavior

Gmail, Yahoo, Outlook—they all behave differently depending on the day and time.

Jenna tested sending the same campaign at:

- 8:00 AM

- 11:00 AM

- 2:00 PM

- 6:00 PM

She learned that her Gmail-heavy segments performed best at 11:00 AM, while Outlook recipients opened more often after lunch.

She used this insight to stagger sends by ISP. Engagement improved. Complaints dropped. Reputation ticked upward.

The Reputation Flywheel

Here's the magic of reputation: it compounds.

High engagement → better inboxing → more engagement → stronger reputation.

Once Jenna built momentum, every campaign got easier. She didn't need to chase open rates. She didn't worry about spam complaints.

She just followed the system:

- Send to the right people

- Use clean design

- Ask for replies

- Track the right metrics

- Adjust based on behavior

The result? A resilient email strategy that didn't rely on hacks.

From Invisible to Irresistible

Six months after nearly giving up on email, Jenna was running some of the best-performing campaigns her company had ever seen.

Her average open rate: 37% Click-through: 4.2% Spam complaint rate: 0.01%

More importantly, she wasn't guessing anymore. She had control. She had insight. She had proof.

Email hadn't changed. She had.

Section Recap: Reputation Is Everything

To land in the inbox in 2025 and beyond, you must:

- Understand how inboxes evaluate you

• Monitor and maintain your sender score

• Clean your list like it's your CRM

• Authenticate your domain fully

• Warm up new IPs gradually

• Use replies as a strategic signal

• Send with rhythm, not randomness

• Design for deliverability, not awards

• Treat your reputation as a living asset

In the next chapter, we'll explore how to write emails that actually get read—now that you know how to make sure they get delivered.

Because a great message is useless if it never arrives.

Chapter 3
Inbox Camouflage:
Design Like a Human, Not a Brand

Section 1: Why Pretty Emails Get Filtered

and Ugly Ones Convert

"Simplicity is the ultimate sophistication."
— Leonardo da Vinci

I f you walk into a coffee shop and someone greets you with a massive light-up billboard that says "SPECIAL OFFER JUST FOR YOU!" you'd probably feel a little weird. But if they smile, hand you a simple note, and say, "Thought you might like this," you're more likely to lean in.

In the inbox, the same principle applies.

Emails that look too much like marketing get treated as marketing. Not just by people, but by the algorithms that protect their inboxes. Fancy designs, bold buttons, banner images, and HTML bells and whistles—they signal "promotion." And promotions get filtered.

That's why some of the most effective emails in the world are the plainest. They look like messages you'd send a colleague. Or a friend. Or yourself.

The Design Trap

Marketers love beautiful things. So they overdesign.

They use brand colors, logos, multiple columns, hero images, callout boxes, button CTAs, and footers with legal disclaimers longer than the email body.

They think design builds trust. But what it really does—in many cases—is scream "mass marketing blast" to inbox filters.

Tools like Gmail and Outlook use machine learning to sort messages. Their job is to protect users from noise. And noisy, overdesigned emails are easy to spot. They trigger rules that route them to the Promotions tab—or worse, to spam.

Meanwhile, a plain-text or lightly formatted email—sent from a real-looking address, written in a conversational tone—gets through. Because it looks like something that matters.

Plain Wins. But Not Boring.

Let's be clear: when we say "plain" we don't mean lifeless. We mean human.

The best-performing emails often use:

- Standard fonts

- No more than one image

- Simple hyperlinks (no buttons)

- One-column layout

- Natural spacing and line breaks

They don't shout. They talk. They don't decorate. They deliver.

And they almost always get better inbox placement, better response rates, and more trust.

Jenna's Shift from Brand to Bare-Bones

Jenna was proud of her email templates. They looked like a high-end SaaS brand: sharp images, gradient buttons, mobile-optimized grids. But her metrics told a different story.

Despite A/B testing subject lines and optimizing CTAs, her click-through rates were stuck below 1%.

Then she sent a plain-text email to a small segment of her list. It was short, personal, and written like a note: "Hey—quick heads-up about a fix we rolled out. Might help you avoid the Gmail tab. Want it? Just reply."

Open rate: 42%. Click-through: 6%. Replies: dozens.

Same list. Same offer. Different approach.

She never looked back.

How Inbox Algorithms Judge Design

Here are common design elements that can hurt deliverability:

• **Multiple images**: Often triggers "promotional" sorting.

• **Buttons**: Especially those styled with CSS or background images.

• **Heavy HTML**: The more code, the more suspicious the message appears.

• **Low text-to-image ratio**: A common spam flag.

• **External tracking scripts**: These can set off alarms.

• **Too many links**: Looks like an affiliate trap.

• **Big logos at the top**: Classic sign of a mass email.

Instead, try this:

• Use raw hyperlinks instead of buttons.

• Keep image use minimal and always include alt text.

• Stick to one-column layouts.

• Limit links to 1–2 per message.

• Write your email in a plain doc before pasting it into your ESP.

Plain Emails Build Trust

People read thousands of emails. Most are trying too hard. When yours doesn't, it stands out. It feels different. It feels real.

That feeling leads to:

- Higher open rates (especially over time)

- More replies (huge for deliverability)

- Lower spam complaints

- Greater loyalty

Your subscribers are busy. They don't want to be marketed to. They want to be spoken to.

Writing in Camouflage

Design isn't just visuals. It's also about tone, formatting, and rhythm.

Here's how to write like a human:

- Use contractions: "you're" not "you are."

- Write in short paragraphs.

- Ask real questions.

- Use lowercase subject lines occasionally.

- Break the grammar rules you'd break in conversation.

Examples:

- "got a sec?"

- "hey—quick favor"

- "this might be a little weird but..."

These don't just look casual. They read casual. And that's the key to breaking through the noise.

Why This Works Today (And Beyond)

In a world of hyper-personalized, AI-generated, over-optimized content, simplicity feels like truth.

The more email becomes automated, the more valuable hand-crafted, real-feeling messages become.

Because while everyone else is trying to impress, you're trying to connect.

That's the power of inbox camouflage.

In the next section, we'll dive into specific formatting tactics, examples, and swipeable frameworks that help your emails look and feel like internal memos—while delivering like million-dollar messages.

Chapter 3 - Section 2

Tactical Camouflage: Formatting Emails That Feel Real (and Still Sell)

When Jenna committed to plain-text style emails, she didn't do it half-heartedly. She knew her audience was used to sleek, branded layouts. Making the switch felt risky. But once she saw the metrics shift—more opens, more replies, and a stronger inbox rate—she realized that human-looking messages weren't just a gimmick. They were a strategy.

The goal of inbox camouflage isn't to trick your audience. It's to make your message feel natural. Non-disruptive. Legitimate. It's the email equivalent of pulling up a chair, not stepping onto a stage.

The Invisible Power of Layout

The layout of an email sends cues long before the content lands.

Massive banners at the top? That's an ad. Two-column grid? That's a newsletter. Large callout boxes? That's a sales push.

But a message that looks like it was typed in Gmail? That's personal.

Here's how to format for authenticity:

1. One Column Only Never use multiple columns. They feel designed and impersonal. Stick to a single vertical column—one flow, one message.

2. Use Basic Fonts Arial, Georgia, Times, or your ESP's default. Fancy fonts not only slow load time but scream "template."

3. Keep Line Width Readable Use a max of 600px. Any wider becomes hard to read. Most ESPs let you set this.

4. Short Paragraphs 1–2 sentences max. Big blocks of text look intimidating. Short paragraphs are easier to skim.

5. Use White Space Intentionally Break things up with spacing. A blank line between every paragraph. Visual relief invites reading.

6. Hyperlinks Over Buttons Plain-text links (underlined blue or not) feel like real communication. Buttons look like marketing.

7. Minimal Images One image max. Ideally below the fold. Always use alt text. No banners, no icons.

8. Avoid Center Alignment Left-aligned text mirrors everyday writing. Centering is rare in personal email.

9. Simple Signature No logos. No legal disclaimers. Just a name, maybe a title, and reply-friendly tone.

Example:

Best, Jenna
Product Marketing, [BrandName]
(P.S. just reply here if you want a copy of the swipe file.)

The Pre-Header Secret

Most people obsess over subject lines. But few think about pre-header text.

Pre-headers are the preview line that shows up next to the subject line in most inboxes. If you don't set one, inboxes will pull the first few lines of your email—which might be messy code or a URL.

Smart marketers write the pre-header intentionally.

• **Bad**: "View this email in your browser"

• **Better**: "Here's something to copy and steal."

• **Best**: "Quick idea for [problem they're facing] (takes 30 seconds)"

The pre-header should complement the subject, not repeat it.

Think of it as your subhead.

Subject Line Formats That Feel Internal

Forget clickbait. These subject line styles feel like internal communication:

- "quick update"

- "couple notes on next week"

- "this might be helpful"

- "heads-up: inbox trick you missed"

- "saw this and thought of you"

- "fast fix for [specific problem]"

These don't overpromise. They build curiosity with restraint.

Real CTA Language That Converts

Instead of: "Shop now," try:

- "Grab yours here"

- "Take a peek"

- "Want to see it?"

- "This might be worth a look"

Instead of: "Read more," try:

- "Here's the full story"

- "I wrote this for you"

- "This hit home—you might like it too"

Instead of: "Reply now," try:

- "What do you think?"

- "Should I send it?"

- "Just reply yes if you want it"

This isn't about tricking people. It's about making every interaction feel like a continuation of a conversation.

The Psychology Behind Plain Emails

We scan our inboxes the same way we scan a room. We're looking for signals of relevance and safety.
Plain emails feel safer. More human. Less like a trap.
Because our brains are wired to notice contrast, and in a sea of polished, overproduced messages, a raw, clean email stands out.
There's also a mirror effect: people write back the way they were written to.

If your email is:

- Formal

- Template-based

- Passive

...you'll get silence or corporate replies.

But if your message is:

- Direct

- Casual

- Emotionally intelligent

...you'll get real engagement.

The "Forwarded Email" Framework

One tactic Jenna used was the "Forwarded Email" format. It mimics the style of someone forwarding a message they found useful.

Subject: "FW: this just helped us 2x replies"

Thought this might help you too. We tried this tweak last week and results were kind of nuts.

--- Forwarded Message --- From: Jenna Blake jenna@yourbrand.com Subject: Re: inbox boost tactic

Short version:

1. Removed images.

2. Used a Gmail-looking format.

3. Asked for a binary reply.

Result: 38% open, 14% reply rate.
LMK if you want to copy the full email.

Why it works:

- Feels urgent

- Looks insider

- Creates curiosity

- Calls back to real tactics

When to Break the Rules

Yes, plain works. But that doesn't mean never use design.

When you've built trust, earned engagement, and your sender reputation is strong, you can layer in:

- Hero images (sparingly)

- Stylized CTAs

- Product carousels (for ecommerce)

- Quote blocks or pull-quotes

- Screenshots, diagrams

But start simple. Earn the right to be fancy.

Jenna's best results came from the emails that looked like they were typed at midnight. Not the ones that looked like agency showpieces.

Case Study: The Ugly Email That Made $110,000

One of Jenna's clients was launching a SaaS tool for freelancers. The team wanted a flashy HTML launch sequence. But after testing,

Jenna convinced them to try something else.

The winning email:

Subject: "want early access?"
Body: hey [first name],
we've been building something for freelancers that takes the worst part of your week (invoicing) and kills it in 3 clicks.
it's in early access.
want in?
just reply yes.
—j

That email generated 600+ replies. Converted at 18%. Revenue: $110,000 in the first two weeks.

It had zero design. No link. No tracking. Just a plain-text message with a compelling offer and a clear CTA.

Inbox Camouflage Isn't Hiding. It's Human.

The goal isn't to trick filters. It's to write in a way that earns your place in the conversation.

By formatting and writing like a human being, you get:

• Better inbox placement

• Stronger engagement

• More trust

• Faster feedback loops

In the next section, we'll go deeper into psychological tactics like curiosity loops, guilt triggers, and conversational CTA phrasing—the tools that make plain emails not just seen, but acted on.

Because camouflage doesn't mean bland. It means blending in long enough to stand out.

Chapter 3 - Section 3

Psychological Camouflage: Writing for Reactoin, Not Just Readability

By now, Jenna had transformed the way she approached every element of her email marketing. Her messages were no longer beautifully branded announcements sent from a faceless company. They were personal, understated, and designed for one thing: authentic connection. The kind that doesn't just get opens or clicks, but earns attention, trust, and action.

But there was one more layer she had to master—and this one wasn't about how an email looked or how it was coded. It was about how it made people feel.

True inbox camouflage isn't only visual. It's psychological.

It uses subtle, persuasive language to bypass the reader's natural defenses. It reads like a message from someone they know. It mirrors the way they think. And it creates emotional momentum so the reader doesn't just read the email—they respond to it.

The Disarming Effect of Vulnerability

Most marketing emails posture. They present polished facts, confident claims, and hyper-optimized statements meant to convert. But the human brain is trained to spot persuasion. And it resists it.

That's why a little vulnerability—even subtle—can go a long way.

Vulnerability in email might look like:

• Admitting uncertainty ("Not sure if this will resonate")

• Owning imperfections ("This email isn't perfect, but I didn't want to wait to send it")

• Sharing personal context ("We tried this out of desperation, and it worked")

Jenna started experimenting with this tone and found that when she showed up a little more human—a little less polished—her reply rates spiked.

She sent a plain note that said:

"Honestly, I'm not even sure this is useful. It helped one of our clients last week, so I figured I'd pass it along."

Replies flooded in.

Why? Because people don't trust perfection. But they lean into honesty.

Creating Conversational Flow

To write emails that feel personal, you have to structure them like a conversation. That means thinking about the rhythm, not just the content.

A good email should:

• Start with a hook that feels like a question or invitation

• Offer just enough context to earn curiosity

• Break the fourth wall and speak directly to the reader

• End with a CTA that feels like a continuation of the discussion

Example:

"hey [first name],
this isn't for everyone. but if your reply rates have been flatlining, this tweak helped us break through last week.
it's super simple. took five minutes to implement.
want me to send it over? just reply yes.
—j"

This doesn't read like marketing. It reads like a tip from a friend. And that's the power of flow.

Use Psychological Patterns That Trigger Micro-Actions

Your email doesn't need to convince someone to buy, book, or subscribe in one go. All it needs to do is move them one step forward.

That might mean:

- Clicking a link

- Replying with a one-word answer

- Opening a future email

- Feeling just curious enough to engage

These micro-actions are cumulative. They build momentum.

To spark them, use language that:

- Frames the action as low risk

- Creates intrigue without being vague

- Makes the reader feel smart for engaging

Examples:

- "Not sure if this is your thing, but..."

- "Most people won't need this. A few will."

- "I made a dumb mistake that actually worked. Want to see it?"

Each phrase respects the reader's autonomy. It doesn't try to force. It invites.

Leaning into Personalization without Tokens

Tokenized personalization (like "Hi [First Name]!") can feel robotic. Instead, aim for situational personalization—referencing where the reader might be in their journey or what problem they're likely wrestling with.

For example:

• "If you're still stuck in the promotions tab, this might help."

• "Still sending image-heavy emails to Gmail? We stopped. Results below."

This shows awareness without guessing wrong or sounding formulaic.

Curiosity Stacking and the Open Loop Effect

Want to keep someone reading? Open a loop. Then stack another. And another.

Instead of:

"Here's the tactic: remove all buttons."

Try:

"We removed one thing from our emails last week. It boosted replies by 19%. But the reason it worked surprised us..."

Now the reader wants to know:

• What did they remove?

• Why did replies go up?

• What was surprising?

That's three open loops—and the more loops you stack (without being manipulative), the more invested your reader becomes.

Empathy-Driven Framing

Camouflage-style emails don't assume interest. They earn it.

That means acknowledging what your reader might be feeling:

• "If you're tired of email advice that sounds like it's from 2006… same."

• "This might feel basic, but it's working better than most advanced tricks."

• "We were skeptical, too. But here's what happened."

Empathy defuses resistance. It shows the reader that you get them. That you're not just pitching—you're listening.

The Loop-Closing CTA

If you open a curiosity loop, you have to close it. But don't just dump the answer—make the reader participate.

Use your CTA to offer closure in exchange for action:

• "Want the full breakdown?"

• "Reply 'framework' and I'll send it."

• "It's not what you think. Happy to send you the case."

This blends curiosity and value with action.

How Emotional Signals Affect Filtering

Most marketers think of spam filters as purely technical. But machine learning algorithms are trained to detect human-like engagement.

That means emotional tone matters.

Emails that:

• Invite responses

• Spark emotional language in replies

• Prompt forwarding or discussion

...get marked as valuable. And value earns better inbox placement.

In other words, writing with emotional intelligence doesn't just connect with people. It teaches the algorithm to respect your messages.

Why Readers Stay Loyal to Real Voices

Once Jenna started writing this way, something surprising happened: people started writing back.

Not just with single-word replies. With full paragraphs.

They said things like:

• "I don't usually reply to these, but this felt like it was meant for me."

• "Honestly, I appreciate how non-pushy your emails are. I actually read them."

• "Thanks for not being annoying. Keep doing what you're doing."

These weren't just nice comments. They were indicators of deep brand affinity.

Jenna learned that her emails had become a signal in their own right—a break from the noise. A reliable voice. A message worth opening.

Section Recap: Psychology Beats Pizzazz

Inbox camouflage isn't about being sneaky. It's about being real.

In this section, we covered how to:

• Use conversational tone to lower resistance

• Deploy curiosity loops that drive action

• Make emotional and empathetic language your strategic advantage

• Use imperfection and humility to build trust

• Personalize without using name tokens

• Stack micro-actions for cumulative engagement

• Write replies that feel like real conversations

Next up, in Chapter 4, we explore the advanced psychology of behaviorally-triggered emails. From gamification to inbox reply traps, to invisible CTAs, you'll learn how to craft emails that don't just get read—they get played with.

Chapter 4

The Psychology of the Click: Behavioral Engagement That Converts

Section 1: Why People Click

(and Why They Don't)

"People don't buy what you do; they buy why you do it."
— Simon Sinek

The click isn't a metric. It's a decision. That might sound obvious, but most email marketers forget it the second they build a campaign. They start thinking in templates, tactics, and tests. They forget that every click comes from a human being with a brain, a mood, a context, a to-do list, and a split second to decide whether your email deserves their attention.

It's not that people don't want to click. It's that you haven't given them a reason that feels worth it.

Jenna learned this the hard way.

She had crafted what she thought was a perfect email: catchy subject line, compelling copy, a bright red button that said "Download Now." But the results were flat. Only 1.2% of readers clicked. Even worse, 6 people unsubscribed.

But when she rewrote the email with one goal—to create *intrigue* instead of pressure—her click-through rate tripled.

What changed? She stopped trying to sell the click.

And she started earning it.

The 3 Elements of a Click-Worthy Email

Every click comes from a combination of three psychological elements:

1. Curiosity: What's on the other side of the click?

2. Safety: Can I trust this won't waste my time or violate my attention?

3. Reward: Will this help me do something better, faster, or easier?

When one of these is missing, the click stalls. When all three are present, it becomes almost irresistible.

Let's break them down.

Curiosity: Opening a Loop You Can't Ignore

Humans are wired to resolve uncertainty. The moment a question is asked, our brains start looking for the answer.

That's why curiosity is one of the most powerful click drivers.

But not all curiosity is created equal.

Low-value curiosity looks like:

• "You won't believe what happened next!"

• "Shocking results from our latest test!"

This is *cheap curiosity*. It works once, then burns trust.

High-value curiosity looks like:

• "This subject line got 4x the clicks (and it breaks every rule we know)."

• "We deleted 60% of our list. Here's what happened."

• "A freelancer's inbox trick that works 8 times out of 10."

This is *earned curiosity*. It rewards the reader for investing attention.

Jenna began writing emails that teased an insight without giving it away. She hinted at transformation. She created just enough tension to make the click feel necessary.

Her rule of thumb became: *Don't create curiosity you can't satisfy. And don't satisfy curiosity you haven't earned.*

Safety: Reducing Click Anxiety

People hesitate to click because they've been burned.

Too many marketers send readers to pages that:

- Auto-play videos

- Trigger pop-ups

- Ask for email addresses again

- Load slowly

- Deliver weak content

Even worse, some clicks result in irrelevant pages or pushy sales funnels. Every bad click trains the brain: "Don't click again."
Smart email marketers reverse this.
They build *click* safety.

This means:

- Set clear expectations ("Here's what you'll see")

- Deliver on the promise

- Make the destination match the message

- Remove surprise barriers (like extra opt-ins)

Jenna started including tiny disclaimers in her CTAs:

- "No sign-up required."

- "2-minute read."

- "Just a PDF—no funnel."

These small signals reduced anxiety. They gave her readers permission to explore.

Reward: Making the Click Feel Like a Win

Every click is a cost. It takes time, attention, energy. People only pay that cost if the return feels worth it.

That return doesn't have to be huge. It can be:

• A simple tactic

• A useful resource

• A moment of entertainment

• A shortcut or framework

What matters is that the reader feels rewarded.

Jenna started rating her own links with this internal question: *Is the value of what's behind this link obvious, fast, and friction-free?*

If it wasn't, she either rewrote the email or didn't link at all. Because one bad click can kill ten good emails.

The CTA Format Shift: From Commands to Choices

The traditional call-to-action says:

• "Click here."

• "Download now."

• "Buy today."

These are commands. And they often trigger resistance.

But choice-based CTAs reframe the click as the reader's idea.

Examples:

- "Want the PDF?"

- "Curious what happened?"

- "Here's the full breakdown if you're into this stuff."

Jenna also started using reply-based CTAs:

"Reply 'framework' if you want the 3-email template."

The replies flooded in. It wasn't just higher engagement. It was *better* engagement.

And every reply boosted her reputation—earning better inbox placement for the next message.

Why Most CTAs Fail (And What to Do Instead)

Most call-to-actions fail for one of three reasons:

1. They feel too pushy.

2. They don't create enough urgency or intrigue.

3. They aren't specific.

Compare:

- "Click here to read more"

- "Get the full story"

• "See how we cut our unsubscribe rate in half"

The third one wins. It creates specificity, reward, and curiosity all at once.

Jenna created a swipe file of high-performing CTAs. Some were link-based, others reply-based. Some were used in the middle of emails, others as PS lines.

Here were a few of her top performers:

• "Want to copy the exact message? I saved it here."

• "Reply with 'yes' and I'll send the whole teardown."

• "This doc saved us 20 hours—worth a peek."

• "You probably don't need this. But if you do...it's here."

These CTAs felt like gifts, not grabs.

The Psychology of Timing

When you make the ask matters. Too early, and it feels presumptuous. Too late, and the reader might tune out.

Jenna found her sweet spot was *just after the first value drop.*

That means:

1. Start with intrigue.

2. Drop one useful insight or idea.

3. Make the ask.

This gives the reader a reason to trust her before she asked for action.

She also tested PS-based CTAs:

• "P.S. The swipe file is ugly, but it works. Want it?"

These performed well because they felt informal—like a tip whispered off-record.

Micro-Commitments and the Ladder of Engagement

Not all clicks are equal. And not all readers are ready for the same level of commitment.

That's why Jenna started building a *ladder of engagement* into her sequences.

Email 1: Ask for a reply (low friction)

Email 2: Link to a short article (moderate friction)

Email 3: Offer a free resource (slightly higher) Email 4: Invite to a free call or purchase (high friction)

By walking readers up the ladder, she warmed them naturally. Each click built confidence. Each action primed the next.

Leveraging Pattern Interrupts

One of Jenna's highest-performing emails started like this:

Subject: "wait...what day is it?"
Body:
"I forgot to send this. No idea how. Maybe you still want it?"

It was quirky. Unpolished. But it worked.

Pattern interrupts work because they disrupt the autopilot behavior of skimming and deleting. They re-engage the brain. They force a pause.

Other examples:

- "This isn't a normal email"

- "I wasn't going to send this. But..."

- "Delete this if you already nailed deliverability"

Each one creates a break in expectation—and that break opens space for curiosity.

Why Click Psychology Drives Deliverability

Clicks aren't just engagement. They're signals.

To inbox providers, a high click-through rate says:

- People care about this sender

- Their emails are useful

- They don't belong in spam

Click behavior is one of the strongest indicators that your emails are relevant.

So when you optimize for real, earned clicks, you're not just boosting conversions. You're improving future inbox placement.

In the next section, we'll break down frameworks and structures for writing high-performance emails—from curiosity stacks to reply triggers to PS-based conversions.

Because now that you understand why people click, it's time to learn exactly how to make them do it consistently.

Chapter 4 - Section 2

Conversion Architecture: Frameworks That Guide the Reader to Action

Once Jenna understood why people clicked, she realized her next challenge: engineering her emails so those clicks weren't just occasional, lucky wins. She needed a consistent, reliable way to move readers from interest to action—without sounding like a marketer, begging for attention, or annoying her list.

She needed structure. Not just intuition.

This section is about the frameworks that do exactly that: structure your emails to maximize behavioral engagement. These are proven blueprints that guide the reader through a micro-journey—from skeptical glance to emotional investment to confident action.

Framework 1: The Curiosity Stack

This is Jenna's go-to when she wants to maximize clicks without hype.

The idea is simple: stack layers of intrigue to open multiple loops the brain wants to close.

Structure:

1. Unexpected subject line

2. Vague but interesting opening

3. Tease a result (without full context)

4. Present a question or choice

5. Offer a soft CTA to resolve the loop

Example:

Subject: "this shouldn't have worked"
Body: we made a change last week that broke every rule we thought

mattered.

response rate jumped 23% overnight.

want the exact copy?

it's weird. but it's working.

click here if you're curious.

Why it works:

• Creates tension early

• Implies a reward

• Lets the reader opt in

You're not yelling for attention. You're planting questions they want answered.

Framework 2: The Problem-Promise-Proof (PPP)

This is the classic conversion structure—but adapted for plain-text, human emails.

1. Problem: Start with a pain point the reader feels

2. Promise: Tease a solution that's simpler than they expect

3. Proof: Share a quick story, stat, or line of logic that validates it

4. CTA: Offer to share more, send a doc, or link to a resource

Example:

Body: everyone talks about open rates. but no one tells you that your cold subscribers are quietly killing deliverability.

we ran a simple reengagement test—then cut 2,400 subs. open rates

went from 14% to 37% in two weeks.
want to see the full sequence? reply "sequence." I'll send it.

Why it works:

- It speaks directly to a real problem

- It offers relief, fast

- It ends with an easy, low-friction ask

PPP is versatile. Use it for:

- Case studies

- Tactics

- Personal stories

- New feature launches

Framework 3: The Decision Tree

This framework gives readers a feeling of agency. You give them a map—and let them choose the path.

Structure:

1. Present 2-3 options

2. Add a sentence of context for each

3. Link or invite a reply for each

Example:

Body: what's your current challenge?

1. not hitting the inbox

2. low reply rates

3. list keeps shrinking

reply with the number and I'll send you a strategy we used to fix it.

Why it works:

- Readers don't feel sold to

- You gather segmentation data from replies

- It scales easily across multiple campaigns

Jenna used this to great effect in onboarding flows, where new subscribers could self-identify their biggest challenge—allowing her to drop them into the right funnel without a single form.

Framework 4: The Minimalist Teardown

Perfect for case studies or postmortems.

1. Start with a result

2. List what you changed

3. Hint at the method

4. Offer to send full breakdown

Example:

Body: 42% open rate. 8.1% replies. here's what we changed:

- moved from html to plain text

- removed all images

- added a binary reply CTA

want the full sequence? reply "reply rate."

Why it works:

- The numbers build credibility

- The bullets are skimmable

- The CTA is a simple action

This works especially well for skeptical audiences who need proof before they trust your advice.

Framework 5: The Soft Follow-Up

Use this when you're continuing a thread or reminding a reader about a previous offer.

Structure:

1. Reference the earlier message

2. Add social proof or a story

3. Invite a soft reply

Example:

Body: sent this last week but didn't want you to miss it.
a few folks replied and saw open rates jump almost instantly.
want me to forward it again?

This doesn't pressure. It respects attention. It keeps you in the reader's world.

Framework 6: The Broken Belief Reframe

Use this when your message challenges conventional wisdom.

Structure:

1. Name the belief

2. Show where it fails

3. Offer a new path

4. Ask if they want to see it

Example:

Body: "send on Tuesdays at 10am" is the worst advice we followed this year.
when we tested sending at 3:17am, open rates jumped 24%.
want to know why?

Why it works:

• Breaks a mental pattern

• Builds curiosity

• Promises insight

These reframes often lead to viral replies—because readers forward them to teammates or friends who share the outdated belief.

How Jenna Used These in a 5-Day Campaign

She designed a five-day launch sequence using one framework per email:

• **Day 1 (Curiosity Stack)**: Introduced a bold, weird stat from a test

• **Day 2 (PPP)**: Shared a short story from a client who doubled reply rates

• **Day 3 (Decision Tree)**: Let readers self-select their pain point

• **Day 4 (Soft Follow-Up)**: Circled back with those who hadn't replied

• **Day 5 (Minimalist Teardown)**: Revealed the full sequence with a final CTA

Result:

- 51% cumulative open rate

- 12% total replies

- 23 booked calls

- Zero spam complaints

She hadn't changed her offer. Just her structure.

Advanced Techniques for CTA Amplification

Once you've chosen a framework, you can add amplification layers:

1. Anchoring

- Contrast your CTA with something harder.

- "No signup. No funnel. Just a PDF."

2. Urgency (without hype)

- "Sending this to 25 people only. Want it?"

- "Closing the loop on this tomorrow. Still want in?"

3. Curiosity Arcs Across Emails

- Tease something in one email that you deliver in the next.

- "More on this Thursday—but this one tweak got us 40% more clicks."

4. Social Proof via Replies

- "Several people replied asking for the doc. Thought I'd send it to you too."

5. Reciprocity Signals

- "We spent 10 hours on this. Hope it saves you 2."

- "Use it, share it, edit it—it's yours."

These don't require heavy copy. Just smart, emotionally intelligent phrasing.

Mistakes to Avoid When Using Frameworks

1. Overusing Curiosity

- If every email is vague, readers stop trusting you.

2. Forcing Urgency

- "Last chance!" every week makes you sound desperate.

3. Being Too Clever

- Clarity beats wit. Don't let wordplay bury your point.

4. Linking Too Early

- Build context before asking for a click.

5. Inconsistent Tone

- Stick with your email voice. Sudden changes kill rapport.

Why These Frameworks Outperform Funnels

Funnels assume the reader is on a path you control. Frameworks respect the reader's attention span and context.

In today's inbox, *flexibility* wins. Frameworks give you just enough structure to write fast, smart emails—without feeling robotic.

Jenna moved from planning 10-email funnels to writing 2-3 emails using these formats. Her campaigns got shorter, sharper, and more profitable.

Section Recap: Don't Just Write Emails. Build Behavioral Journeys.

Here's what we covered:

- Why frameworks create structure without sounding formulaic

- Six high-conversion email structures for different goals

- How to amplify CTAs with psychological nuance

- Mistakes to avoid that kill engagement

- How Jenna used this approach to engineer her most successful launch ever

Next up: in Section 3, we'll explore how to embed gamification into email campaigns—using interactivity, mini-challenges, and reply loops that drive ongoing engagement and make subscribers *want* to participate.

Because the only thing better than a click is a reader who keeps coming back for more.

Chapter 4 - Section 3

Email as a Game: Gamification and Interactivity for Lasting Engagement

By now, Jenna had a list that opened, read, and clicked. But she noticed something else: many subscribers engaged once, then disappeared. The solution wasn't to send more emails. It was to make her emails more fun.

This wasn't about adding graphics or building HTML puzzles. It was about using behavioral psychology and game design principles to turn every email into a tiny, interactive experience—one that rewarded readers for participating, invited them into feedback loops, and created momentum.

Gamification isn't just for apps. It's a secret weapon for marketers who understand attention is a currency—and engagement is a habit.

What Is Gamification in Email?

Gamification in email means adding game-like elements to encourage interaction.

That could look like:

- Scoring systems

- Challenges or prompts

- Poll-style reply choices

- Unlockable resources

- Reply incentives

But it's more than novelty. It's behavioral design.

Games work because they:

- Offer a clear goal

- Provide feedback

- Reward progress

- Tap into curiosity and competition

Jenna started treating each email like a micro-game. A single decision point. A way for readers to play.

Behavioral Triggers from Game Design

1. Variable Rewards

- Not every email gives a reward.

- Some replies unlock docs. Others just thank the reader.
- This randomness increases dopamine.

2. Streak Tracking

- Jenna used language like "You're 2-for-2 on replies this week. Want to keep it going?"

- It created continuity.

3. Personalized Quests

- "Want a list-building checklist or a cold-subscriber script? Reply 1 or 2."

- Readers got to choose their path.

4. Social Proof & Leaderboards

- "First 50 replies get early access."

• "Top engagers this week got this PDF."

These elements turned her list into a light community—without any tech stack.

Gamified CTA Structures

Instead of:

• "Click here to download."

Try:

• "Want the doc? Solve this: What word do you think gets 2x more replies than 'yes'?"

Instead of:

• "Reply if you want the checklist."

Try:

• "Reply with the emoji that matches your current inbox mood [list emojis]. I'll send you a resource based on your answer."

Readers didn't just click. They played. And that made Jenna's emails something people looked forward to—not just tolerated.

Gamified Series Example: The 5-Day Challenge

Jenna designed a mini email series around engagement-building.

Day 1: Opt-In Prompt
Subject: "Want a 5-day reply rate boost?"
Body:

"I'm running a 5-day challenge. Super low time. Super high ROI. Each day: 1 idea, 1 action. Reply YES to join."

Day 2: Challenge Begins

Task: Remove 10% of your coldest subs.
Reward: A re-engagement script if they do it.

Day 3: CTA Test

Task: Swap your button for a hyperlink.
Mini-vote: "Reply HYPER if you did it."

Day 4: Obscure Tactic

Task: Add a PS line with a second CTA.
CTA: "Reply with your PS idea, and I'll send ours."

Day 5: Unlock Bonus

Subject: "Only for those who played..."
Body: "You made it. Reply WINNER and I'll send you the PDF with all five strategies, plus two bonus ones."

Results:

- 31% opt-in on Day 1

- 44% engagement on Day 3

- 19% of participants replied to all five emails

- Dozens of replies on Day 5 asking for more challenges

Jenna wasn't sending emails anymore. She was building habits.

Gamification Without Tech

You don't need fancy plugins. You need:

- A compelling prompt

- A sense of progress

- A reason to respond

- Optionality

Simple gamification ideas:

- Choose Your Own Adventure: Let readers decide what to get next.

- Reply Tiers: Reply once = doc. Reply three times = bonus resource.

- Mystery Unlocks: "Next week, something special. But only if you opened 2 of the last 3 emails."

Jenna used UTM tracking + Mailgun open data to segment engaged readers. But you can use ESP filters or manual tags.

Psychological Advantages of Gamification

1. Limbic Resonance

- Games tap the emotional brain. Less logic, more feeling.

2. Narrative Immersion

- Readers become part of the story. They're not just being told—

they're playing.

3. Feedback Loops

 • Every action gets a result. Even a thank-you email is reinforcement.

4. Micro-Dopamine Hits

• Unlocking something triggers satisfaction. That satisfaction leads to retention.

Gamified emails stop being background noise. They become a highlight.

The Art of Mystery

Jenna found that mystery was the most reliable driver of engagement.

She used these techniques:

• Redacted subject lines: "[Something] is killing your reply rate"

• Blurred CTAs: "I could explain it... but it's easier if I just show you."

• Delayed reveals: "I'll show you the results tomorrow. Today, just do this."

Mystery doesn't have to be manipulative. It has to be *meaningful*.

Trigger-Based Games

You can turn any behavior into a game:

• **Open Triggers**: "If you opened yesterday's email, this one's for you."

• **Click Triggers**: "You clicked. That says something. Here's part two."

• **Reply Triggers**: "I owe you the resource. But I added something extra."

These feel earned. And earned engagement is the strongest kind.

Examples of Gamified CTAs That Worked

1. "Reply with one word: DELETE or KEEP. I'll tell you if we agree."

2. "Pick one: STRATEGY, STORY, or STATS. I'll send you what you pick."

3. "Want to win a weird prize? Just reply with the last subject line I sent."

Even without a literal prize, the act of playing created loyalty.

Why It Feels Like a Conversation

Games are reciprocal. You do something. The world responds. Good email campaigns mimic this.

Every click, reply, open becomes part of a living loop:

• Reader acts

• You respond

• They expect it next time

This builds what Jenna called "micro-rituals" — little moments that repeat, build trust, and become part of the reader's inbox routine.

Scaling Without Losing the Magic

Worried this only works for small lists?

Jenna scaled to 40,000 subs by:

• Using automated replies for each trigger (pre-written, natural tone)

• Batch-segmenting based on replies (using tags or filters)

• Offering general content when specifics weren't scalable

• Celebrating top engagers publicly

Gamification isn't about being custom. It's about being human.

Unexpected Bonuses That Build Loyalty

One of Jenna's favorite tactics was the *surprise* follow-up. If someone replied with a codeword (e.g. "INBOX"), they got a doc.

Three days later, they got another message:

"You didn't ask for this, but I thought you'd like it."

That message contained a bonus: a one-line swipe file, or a testimonial from someone using the tactic. Readers felt seen. Valued. Part of something.
And they stayed subscribed.

Gamified Referral Email

Subject: "Want to unlock the referral vault?"
Body:
Here's the deal:
Share this email with one person who writes email copy. If they subscribe, I'll send you our referral vault.
No codes. No trackers. Just shoot me a screenshot if they opt in.

Simple. Low-tech. Effective.

The Anti-Gamification Philosophy

Sometimes the best game is no game.

Every 4–5 emails, Jenna sent a plain message:

"No tricks. Just a doc we built that might help. Want it?"

This contrast amplified her more playful emails. It signaled respect. It reminded people she wasn't just trying to entertain—she was trying to help.

Section Recap: Turn Engagement Into a Habit

Gamification works when:

- You invite participation

- You reward effort

- You use feedback to create momentum

- You respect your reader's time

From simple reply-based games to multi-day challenges, gamified emails deepen connection, boost deliverability, and build anticipation.

Next up: Chapter 5. We'll dig into list building strategies that attract high-quality, engaged subscribers from the beginning—so your inbox games and conversion frameworks land with the right audience from day one.

Chapter 5

The List Is the Leverage:

Building Audiences That Actually Engage

Section 1: Why the Wrong List

Ruins the Right Strategy

"Your most unhappy customers are your greatest source of learning."
— Bill Gates

There's an uncomfortable truth in email marketing that most professionals avoid talking about: You can do everything right—great copy, strong offers, a bulletproof infrastructure—and still get dismal results if your list isn't right.

It doesn't matter how polished your email is if it's landing in the inbox of someone who never wanted to hear from you in the first place. It doesn't matter how clear your CTA is if the reader never really needed what you were offering. Engagement starts long before the first open. It starts the moment someone decides to give you their email address.

Jenna had learned this the hard way. After months of optimizing her email templates, rebuilding her reputation, and gamifying her campaigns, she hit a plateau. Her opens started to stagnate. Her reply rates dipped. People weren't unsubscribing in droves, but they weren't participating either. It was like shouting into a well and hearing your own voice echo back.

So she did something radical. She audited the list itself.

What she discovered changed her entire approach to email.

Where Bad Lists Come From

Jenna's email list had grown steadily over time. It came from a mix of content downloads, lead magnets, webinar signups, sales calls, networking events, and trade show promotions. On paper, it looked healthy. Big numbers. Diverse sources.

But when she segmented her list by original source and engagement behavior, the pattern was painfully clear: most of her engaged subscribers had come from only a few channels. The rest had inflated her numbers without adding value.

That's when she realized: not all growth is good growth.

The truth is, there are three types of list growth:

• **Vanity Growth**: Feels impressive, but adds no long-term engagement. Usually from giveaways, contests, co-branded events.

• **Passive Growth**: Happens through forms, blog traffic, SEO. Usually slow and variable in quality.

• **Intentional Growth**: Comes from strategic content, aligned offers, and systems designed to attract high-fit subscribers.

Jenna's list had too much vanity, too much passive, and not enough intentional.

The Cost of a Bad Subscriber

Every disengaged subscriber costs you twice.

First, they dilute your engagement rates—lowering your open averages, damaging your sender reputation, and putting future sends at risk.

Second, they distort your data. You start testing subject lines or CTAs and making decisions based on the behavior of people who were never a good fit in the first place.

Jenna calculated that nearly 40% of her list hadn't opened an email in the last 120 days. Those people weren't prospects. They were ballast.

She made the decision to cut 4,800 names in one day.

It was terrifying.

And it was the best move she ever made.

Her open rate jumped from 19% to 34%. Reply rates doubled. Deliverability issues disappeared. It was like giving her email engine a full oil change.

Why Most Lead Magnets Don't Work

The most common method for growing an email list is the lead magnet. You create a free resource, ask for an email in exchange, and grow your list one download at a time.

But most lead magnets are built to get opt-ins, not build relationships.

They offer:

- High-perceived value, low practical use

- Broad appeal, weak qualification

- Irrelevant follow-up content

The result is a list of people who wanted the resource, but not the relationship.

Jenna had a lead magnet that got thousands of downloads—a massive PDF with 50 email subject lines. But the people who downloaded it rarely engaged with her content afterward.

So she tested something new: a short, plain-text "toolkit" emailed directly after opt-in, with a clear invitation to reply and ask questions.

It got half the opt-ins. But five times the engagement.

Designing a Magnet for Engagement, Not Just Emails

To create a lead magnet that fuels long-term engagement, Jenna applied three principles:

1. Relevance: The magnet should solve a problem closely related to the content she wanted to send later. If you sell email deliverability tools, your lead magnet shouldn't be "50 AI Prompt Templates."

2. Velocity: The magnet should offer a quick win—something the reader can apply or benefit from within 5 minutes. Long reports are ignored. Short wins get remembered.

3. Conversation Triggers: The magnet should create a reason for the subscriber to reply. That reply builds reputation, and more importantly, it creates the start of a relationship.

Her best-performing lead magnet was just a 1-page checklist with 10 inbox deliverability tips. At the end of the checklist, she added this line:

P.S. Which of these are you NOT doing? Hit reply and let me know. I might have something extra for you.

Nearly 17% of new subscribers replied. That single line changed everything.

The Myth of the Massive List

In an industry obsessed with scale, there's a myth that more subscribers means more power. But that assumes every subscriber is equally valuable.

They're not.

Jenna proved this when she launched a new offer to two lists:

• List A: 40,000 subs, average open rate 18%

• List B: 4,200 subs, average open rate 46%

Revenue:

• List A: $11,700

• List B: $27,900

List B was smaller, but it was built intentionally. Every person on it had engaged in the last 45 days. Every message felt like a continuation, not a broadcast.

From that day forward, Jenna stopped saying "grow the list." She started saying "build the audience."

How to Audit Your Existing List

Before trying to grow your list, clean it.

Jenna ran a full audit using these questions:

- Who hasn't opened in 90+ days?

- Which sources produce subscribers who stay engaged?

- Which sources produce ghost subscribers?

- What segments reply?

- What patterns predict unsubscribes?

She built a segmentation system:

- **Active**: Opened in last 30 days

- **Warming**: Opened 31-90 days ago

- **Inactive**: 90+ days, no engagement

She stopped sending to the Inactive segment completely. No reengagement campaigns. Just cold suppression.

This small shift drastically improved her sender score, and inbox rates followed.

The Opt-In Flow That Signals Quality

Jenna redesigned her opt-in flow with friction—on purpose. Instead of a splashy landing page with a headline and bullet points, she wrote a plain-text letter explaining what subscribers would receive and how often. Then she added a checkbox:

Yes, I want to receive practical, plain-text tips about inbox engagement. I know I can unsubscribe anytime.

It reduced opt-ins by 18%.

But the subscribers who came through that gate? They opened at 52% and replied 11% of the time.
Permission is powerful.

Why Paid Ads Usually Create Bad Lists

Most paid acquisition for list building leads to poor-quality subscribers.
Jenna tested Facebook, Google, and Twitter ads. The cost-per-lead was attractive. But the downstream engagement was miserable.

She realized:

• People who opt-in passively are less invested.

• Cold audiences don't trust you yet.

• Most ad traffic is designed to optimize clicks, not conversations.

Instead, she shifted her ad strategy to drive traffic to content first. Not an opt-in. Not a lead magnet. Just a useful article.

Then, within the article, she embedded a signup form with this CTA:

Want more like this? I send tips every Tuesday. No fluff. No graphics. Just stuff that works.

It got lower volume. But better subscribers.

Building Lists from High-Intent Conversations

Jenna also began collecting emails in non-traditional ways:

- At the end of podcast interviews

- From DMs on LinkedIn

- From webinar chat follow-ups

- From replies to cold emails that went well

Each time, she personally invited the person to join her list:

"Hey—totally optional, but I send out 1-2 emails a week with stuff like we talked about. Want in?"

Her conversion rate was 70%+—and those people became her most responsive readers.

Section Recap: Your List Is a System, Not a Trophy

If the wrong subscribers are on your list, no amount of clever writing will save you. And if the right ones are there, even your simplest emails will work.

Here's what we covered:

- Why list quality trumps list size

- How most lead magnets attract the wrong people

- How to design an opt-in that signals fit

• Why engagement should shape every acquisition strategy

• How Jenna rebuilt her list from the inside out

In Section 2, we'll break down the psychology of audience-building—how to attract, filter, and nurture the kinds of readers who trust you from day one.

Because great email isn't about what you send. It's about who's waiting to hear from you.

Chapter 5 - Section 2

The Psychology of Attraction: How to Draw the Right People to Your List

Most list-building strategies start with tactics: landing pages, opt-in forms, lead magnets. But these are only as powerful as the psychological magnetism behind them. Jenna didn't rebuild her list by redesigning forms. She rebuilt it by changing who she spoke to, how she spoke to them, and why they chose to listen.

This section is about audience psychology. If Section 1 was about removing friction from the wrong people, this is about creating gravity for the right ones.

Attention Is Earned, Not Captured

Jenna used to believe that the job of a headline was to grab attention. Now she believes it's to deserve it.

Every potential subscriber is already drowning in messages. The inbox is crowded. So is social media. And so is their head.

To stand out, you don't need to be louder. You need to feel more relevant.

That starts with resonance.

The Reader's Internal Monologue

When a potential subscriber sees your email, your ad, your opt-in form, or your content, they're not thinking:

"Wow, what an amazing copywriter."

They're thinking:

"Do I trust this person to help me with the thing I'm wrestling with?"

If the answer is yes, they give you their email. If the answer is no, they scroll.

Jenna learned to ask a new question when writing opt-in copy:

"What conversation is already happening in their head that I can join?"

She stopped trying to write persuasive headlines. She started trying to write familiar thoughts.

Mirroring vs Marketing

Marketing is about persuasion. Mirroring is about recognition.

Mirroring looks like:

• Naming the problem exactly as they feel it

• Using the language they use (not industry terms)

• Starting where they already are

Instead of:

"Boost your email ROI with automation"

Try:

"If you're tired of emails getting ignored, here's what to change."

This feels like understanding, not selling. That creates emotional safety—which creates permission.

What the Right Subscriber Feels at Signup

When someone signs up for the right reason, they feel:

• Understood

• Curious

• Relieved

• Hopeful

They're not thinking, "Sweet, another newsletter." They're thinking, "Maybe this person can help."

Jenna started using language like:

"This list isn't for everyone. But if you care about inboxing better emails that people actually reply to, you'll like it here."

She wasn't just trying to attract subscribers. She was trying to filter for fit.

The Principle of Self-Selection

Every good email list filters people in and out.

Jenna created opt-ins that invited readers to decide for themselves:

"I send simple, plain-text, no-BS ideas about email that works in 2025. Want in?"

People who wanted fancy design? They bounced. People who liked the tone? They joined.

The result: smaller list. Higher trust.

How Tone Creates Fit

List-building is tone-building.

If your signup tone is hypey, you'll attract hype-chasers. If your tone is snarky, you'll attract snark. If your tone is thoughtful, you'll attract reflection.

That means the way you say things matters as much as what you say.

Jenna made her opt-ins sound like her emails:

- Casual

- Curious

- Direct

- Helpful

That created continuity—which built trust before the first email even landed.

Creating Magnetic Positioning

Jenna used to say, "I help people write better emails." Now she says, "I help good emails land where they belong—the inbox."

That shift did three things:

1. Made her distinct

2. Made her useful

3. Made her memorable

Magnetic positioning isn't about being clever. It's about being specific.

The best lead magnet headline Jenna ever wrote was:

"You don't need better subject lines. You need better readers."

That line alone drove hundreds of high-fit subscribers because it filtered for people who had tried all the basic tricks and were ready for something deeper.

Speak to Beliefs, Not Just Pain

Most marketers focus on pain points. Jenna started focusing on beliefs.

Instead of:

"Struggling to get replies?"

Try:

"If you believe email still works, this list is for you."

Belief-based copy attracts higher-fit subscribers because it builds identity.

People want to join communities that reflect who they are or who they aspire to be.

Your list is a club. Say the name of the club out loud.

Psychological Anchors That Build Long-Term Readers

1. The Promise of Consistency

- "I send every Tuesday. No fluff."

- Creates reliability.

2. The Value Statement

- "One idea. One example. Every time."

• Sets expectations.

3. The Connection Cue

• "This list is small on purpose."

• Signals intimacy.

These anchors reduce uncertainty—which reduces churn.

Why Scarcity Still Works (If It's Honest)

Jenna experimented with limiting list access.

On a webinar, she said:

"I'm opening up my private email list to 100 new people this week. Then it's closed."

She meant it. She manually closed the form after 100 signups.

The result:

• 89% of new subs opened the first email

• 38% replied

• Dozens became clients

Scarcity is powerful. But only if it's real.

Avoiding Audience Contamination

The wrong subscribers change your writing.

If you start optimizing for engagement from the lowest-common denominator, you write:

• Shorter emails (because people don't read)

• Flashier subject lines (because attention is low)

• Simpler offers (because trust is missing)

Instead, Jenna decided to raise the bar. She said, "I write long emails. If you're still reading, you're my kind of person."

That created a filter. A feedback loop. And a list of people who leaned in.

How to Attract Readers Who Stay

Here's what Jenna changed to improve retention from day one:

• **Welcome Email**: No pitch. Just story. Why the list exists. What to expect.

• **Ask a Question**: Prompt a reply immediately. Builds the habit.

• **Set the Tone**: Subject line: "This is not a newsletter."

• **First Resource**: High value, low hype. A checklist that solved a problem.

• **Second Email**: Referenced replies from the first. Created community.

This isn't automation. It's onboarding. And it doubled her 30-day engagement rate.

What Jenna Wrote in Her New Opt-In Page

Instead of flashy copy, she wrote this:

You're busy. The inbox is crowded.
I write emails about writing emails that actually get read. And replied to. And acted on.
You won't get graphics, discounts, or fluff.
You'll get ideas that work.
If that sounds useful, drop your email. If not, that's fine too.

It didn't go viral.
But the people who signed up?

• Stayed longer

• Replied more

• Bought faster

Section Recap: Pull, Don't Push

To build a high-fit email list, you need more than a magnet. You need a philosophy.

That means:

• Writing like you respect attention

• Speaking to real beliefs, not just pain

• Mirroring your reader's voice, not marketing over them

• Letting tone and positioning filter for fit

• Onboarding readers with context and care

In Section 3, we'll explore specific acquisition channels—which ones actually produce high-engagement readers, and how Jenna designed entry points that amplified trust instead of eroding it.

Because building a powerful list isn't just about who joins. It's about how they arrive.

Chapter 5 - Section 3

Channels That Create Connection: Designing Entry Points That Scale Trust

J enna had rewritten her lead magnet. She had clarified her positioning. Her tone was consistent. Her open and reply rates were climbing. But she hit another wall. The problem wasn't who was signing up. The problem was where they were coming from.

She was still spending time on podcasts, partnerships, SEO, organic posts, the occasional webinar. But her results were inconsistent. Some weeks brought in subscribers who engaged deeply. Others brought in a flood of tire-kickers.

She realized she needed to do what few email marketers ever do: design her acquisition channels with as much thought as her emails themselves.

This section is about sourcing subscribers intentionally. It's about building a system where every entry point pre-qualifies, primes, and prepares someone to become not just a reader, but a participant.

Most Channels Focus on Volume, Not Fit

The typical marketing advice is to diversify traffic. Be everywhere. Create omnipresence. But omnipresence without intentionality builds bloated lists. Not effective ones.

Jenna started mapping her lead sources to actual engagement metrics:

• Time on list

• Open rate

• Reply rate

• Click-to-open rate

• Conversion (if applicable)

Then she reverse-engineered what the top-performing subscribers had in common.

The answer wasn't what she expected.

It wasn't just the source. It was the context in which they discovered her.

Context is the Conversion Catalyst

A subscriber who finds you through a retweeted thread is not the same as one who finishes a 45-minute podcast and joins your list.

They differ in:

- Trust

- Attention span

- Expectations

- Willingness to engage

That's why Jenna stopped measuring channels by top-of-funnel volume. She started measuring by downstream depth.

Designing for Intent, Not Impressions

She built a simple quadrant:

- **High Intent, High Context**: Podcast listeners, webinars, personal referrals

- **High Intent, Low Context**: Targeted Google SEO, deep Twitter threads

- **Low Intent, High Context**: Casual co-branded events, summits

• **Low Intent, Low Context**: Cold ads, giveaways, generic traffic

Then she made a decision: only focus on the top two.

That meant she prioritized channels where people showed up on purpose, and left feeling like they knew her.

Podcast Appearances as Entry Points

Jenna had underestimated podcasts. She saw them as awareness plays. But when she ended an episode with a direct, human CTA, everything changed.

"If you liked this, I send plain-text ideas about what actually works in email. It's not a newsletter. It's a conversation. You can join at [URL]."

Suddenly, her subscribers from podcasts:

• Opened 60% of her emails

• Replied more often

• Forwarded more frequently

• Stayed subscribed longer

She doubled down, not just appearing on more shows, but being more intentional:

• She prepped hosts with stories tied to her opt-in.

• She made the call-to-action feel like an extension of the episode.

• She followed up with every host, and sent them the results.

The result: dozens of podcast subscribers became customers

within 30 days.

Owned Content Hubs That Prime Subscribers

Instead of using landing pages as catch-alls, Jenna created a content hub—a curated series of posts, videos, and short resources that introduced her philosophy.

It wasn't optimized for conversion. It was optimized for understanding.

Her content hub included:

• A plain explainer on sender reputation

• A teardown of one of her best-performing email sequences

• An interactive tool for grading your last subject line

At the end of each piece was the same invitation:

"If this made you rethink how you use email, I send a note every Tuesday with stuff like this."

The opt-in rate? 3-5x higher than her main site. Engagement? Some of the best on her list.

The Power of Content Before the Capture

Jenna realized most lead-gen strategies try to capture attention first, then deliver value.

She flipped it.

She gave the value first. In full. For free.

Only after someone had *experienced* her ideas would she invite them to subscribe.

This flipped the power dynamic. Instead of begging for a signup, she was offering a way to keep going.

"If this helped, I send more. Join if you want."

No hard sell. No pop-ups. Just trust.

Partnerships That Pre-Qualify

Jenna stopped partnering with people just because they had big lists.

She created a checklist:

- Does their audience share my belief in email as a trust channel?

- Do they send plain-text or over-designed messages?

- Have they actually engaged with my content?

Then she offered value-first partnerships:

- Co-write an email for their list

- Create a shared toolkit (with no squeeze page)

- Appear on a live Q&A

At the end, she made this ask:

"If this conversation resonated, and you want more practical stuff like this, I share it here."

Partners were shocked. It converted better than most webinars. Because it didn't feel like a funnel. It felt like a natural next step.

Social Content That Filters

Instead of chasing likes, Jenna used social to qualify.

Every post had one goal: attract readers who already agreed with her philosophy.

She said things like:

- "Open rate isn't a KPI. It's a lagging indicator of trust."

- "Email without replies is just digital shouting."

- "Your email list isn't a list. It's a relationship index."

These weren't designed to go viral. They were designed to filter.

Then, in the comments or replies, she dropped this line:

"If this sounds like your kind of inbox, I send more at [URL]."

The people who clicked were almost always a match.

Webinars That Convert (Because They Teach)

Jenna had run dozens of webinars before. Most were forgettable. Then she flipped the format.

Instead of a slide deck, she:

- Started with a teardown of a real email

- Made the chat active immediately ("Reply with your open rate")

- Gave real-time advice

• Pitched only in the last 5 minutes

At the end, she said:

"This list is where I share what I can't fit into slides. No templates. Just tested stuff. You're welcome to join."

Her list grew slower. But stronger.

Cold Traffic That Works (Rarely)

Jenna still tested paid channels, but with one rule:

• No lead magnet until trust is built.

She ran ads to free articles. No opt-ins. No tracking.

At the end of each article was this:

"If this changed how you think about email, there's more where this came from. [Opt-in link]"

Cost per subscriber was higher. But 2-3x better downstream engagement.

Referral Loops That Reward Trust

Jenna added this to the bottom of her emails:

"If you know someone who writes email and hates most email advice, forward this to them. They can join here."

It felt personal. It worked.
She tracked referral source in her ESP. Referred subscribers had higher open and reply rates.

Then she added a twist:

• Anyone who referred 3+ people got a private doc (manually sent).

This created quiet buzz—not big viral spikes, but steady, qualified growth.

Building Entry Point Sequences

For each acquisition channel, Jenna built a short sequence:

• **Welcome Email**: Match the tone of where they found her

• **Story Email**: Why this work matters

• **Interactive Email**: Prompt a reply or a click

• **Deep Value Email**: Deliver a full teardown or framework

This turned every new subscriber into a warmed reader within 72 hours.

Why Entry Points Are More Important Than Lead Magnets

Jenna realized something profound: most marketers obsess over what happens after someone subscribes.
But the decision to subscribe is shaped entirely by the 10 seconds before it.

• What did they just hear?

• What did they just read?

• How do they feel about you?

• What story are they telling themselves?

Get that right, and everything else is easier.

Section Recap: Source Matters More Than Size

If you want a list that engages, you need entry points that pre-engage.

Here's what we covered:

• Why high-fit subscribers are shaped by where they come from

• How context influences conversion more than copy

• Why podcasts, content hubs, and partnerships drive deeper trust

• How to build referral systems and cold traffic filters that actually work

• Why every channel needs a short onboarding sequence to sustain momentum

With the right list-building channels, you don't need a massive list. You need a small group of people who actually care.

In Chapter 6, we'll go deep on retention: how to keep subscribers engaged for the long term, build rituals, and turn your email into a habit readers don't want to break.

Chapter 6
Make It a Habit:
Turning Readers Into
Lifelong Subscribers

Section 1: The Hidden Art of Retention

"We are what we repeatedly do. Excellence, then, is not an act, but a habit."
— Aristotle

When Jenna looked at her analytics, she noticed something odd. Her unsubscribes weren't high, but her engagement curve had a steep drop-off. New subscribers would open, click, sometimes reply—but then slowly fade into silence. They didn't unsubscribe. They just stopped caring.

And that, she realized, was a bigger problem.

Because losing attention is more dangerous than losing subscribers. When someone unsubscribes, you have clarity. But when someone ghosts? You keep emailing into the void, hurting your deliverability and misreading your real reach.

Jenna knew how to get attention. She knew how to earn the click. Now she had to learn something much harder: how to keep attention over time.

This is where most email marketers lose. Not at the first open. Not at the opt-in. But at week four, or five, or six—when the novelty wears off, and the message becomes background noise.

So she set out to design an email strategy that people didn't just tolerate, but look forward to.

Email as Ritual, Not Content

The first shift was conceptual. Jenna stopped thinking of her emails as "content." That word made her think of value, length, formatting.

Instead, she started thinking about them as *rituals*.

A ritual is something you come back to. Something familiar, but evolving. Something that anchors a day, a week, a rhythm.

She asked herself, "What would make this email something people expect, miss, and maybe even talk about if it didn't show up?"

That question led to an entirely new architecture.

Consistency Isn't Just for Algorithms

Everyone says you should be consistent in email. Most say it's because of inbox algorithms. But Jenna learned that consistency is more powerful because of reader psychology.

When people know when to expect your message, they start to associate it with that moment.

Tuesday morning. Thursday afternoon. End of month.

Your email becomes a part of their mental map. That familiarity reduces friction. It builds trust, even before the message is read.

Jenna picked a rhythm: Tuesday mornings. She stuck with it. Her audience adapted. Her engagement stabilized.

But consistency wasn't enough.

The Role of Signature Structure

Jenna noticed her best emails had a similar shape:

- A short, personal intro

- A simple insight or observation

- A practical takeaway

- A soft sign-off or invitation

She decided to stop reinventing the wheel. She leaned into that structure—not as a formula, but as a framework.

Readers began to recognize the flow. They knew what to expect. And that made the message easier to read—and easier to remember.

The takeaway? People return to formats they trust.

The Familiar + The Unexpected

Jenna realized retention lives in the tension between the expected and the surprising.

If an email is too consistent—same voice, same format, same rhythm—it becomes skippable. Predictability becomes monotony.

But if every email is different, you lose identity.

She found a middle path. Familiar voice. Reliable rhythm. But a rotating mix of content types:

• One week: a story

• Next week: a teardown

• Then: a framework or list

This variety kept readers engaged, without losing cohesion. It wasn't about novelty. It was about freshness.

Personalization That Doesn't Scale (But Matters Anyway)

Jenna started replying to every 10th subscriber who replied to her. Not with a template. With a real answer, or thank-you, or question.

This didn't scale. But it resonated.

Those readers kept opening. Some became clients. Others became advocates.

Even more powerful? She started referencing prior replies in future emails:

"Last week, someone asked if subject lines even matter anymore. Here's what I told them."

Suddenly, the list felt like a group chat. Not a broadcast.

Replays, Recaps, and Recirculation

Not every reader opens every email. But every email costs you deliverability if it lands silently.

So Jenna started recirculating.

Once a quarter, she sent a "highlight reel"—her top three emails, rewritten slightly, with new headlines and fresh framing.

She also built a library page where subscribers could browse her top ideas. Not a blog. A curated archive.

Then she linked to it in every welcome email:

"If you're new here, these are the five ideas people come back to most."

It became her most clicked link. More than any lead magnet. More than any offer.

The Drop-Off Recovery Plan

Every list loses people. But Jenna decided not to lose them quietly. She set up a drop-off reactivation sequence.

If someone hadn't opened in 45 days, they got this email:

Subject: "Still with me?"
Body:
"You haven't opened in a while. That's totally okay. I'd rather send fewer emails to the people who still care. If that's you, click here and I'll keep you in. If not, no hard feelings. I'll quietly remove you."

This reactivated about 8% of readers. But more importantly, it let Jenna protect her list quality without a full purge.

Why Most Retention Strategies Fail

Here's what Jenna learned: most email retention fails not because of unsubscribes, but because of stagnation.

Marketers stop trying once a subscriber joins. They send value. They send updates. They send promotions.

But they forget to build a relationship.

Jenna began treating her list like a network of individuals. Not just numbers.

She asked herself before every send:

- Does this continue a conversation?

- Does this deepen trust?

- Would I want to open this?

Retention isn't a strategy. It's a commitment.

Section Recap: Keep the Ones You Earned

Retention is the difference between growth and churn. It's how small lists win big. And how great email marketers stay great.

In this section, we covered:

- How ritual thinking creates anticipation

- Why consistency builds familiarity, and structure builds memory

- The power of soft personalization and real replies

- How recirculating content keeps messages from going stale

- What a simple reactivation can do for long-term engagement

In Section 2, we'll dig into behavioral segmentation—how to read the signals your audience is sending, and how to speak to readers at exactly the right moment, in the right tone, with the right message.

Because retention isn't just about showing up. It's about showing up differently for different people.

Chapter 6 - Section 2

Segmenting for Relevance: How to Keep Attention by Speaking to Behavior

Retention doesn't begin with a better message. It begins with the right message for the right person at the right time. Jenna used to treat her email list as one audience. Same emails. Same cadence. Same language. The results were solid—but something felt off. She'd get confused replies, quiet opt-outs, and unpredictable engagement.

Then she had a realization that changed everything: her list wasn't one audience. It was several different kinds of readers living inside one inbox.

Each reader had a different story. Different goals. Different levels of trust. And unless she acknowledged that, she would eventually lose all of them.

So she stopped writing to her list and started writing for her segments.

The First Rule: Behavior Is the Best Signal

Demographics tell you who someone is. Behavior tells you who they're becoming.

When Jenna looked at her metrics, she didn't just see clicks. She saw questions:

- Who clicked once and never again?

- Who opened every email but never replied?

- Who replied instantly with questions, then went silent?

- Who forwarded her emails to others?

Each behavior was a signal—a breadcrumb.
Jenna began mapping her list into live behavioral segments.

Segment 1: The Warm Actives These were her loyal readers. They opened within 24 hours. They clicked links. They replied. Some even forwarded.

For these subscribers, Jenna sent:

- Behind-the-scenes insights

- Personal stories

- Exclusive early access offers

These readers didn't need proof. They needed reward. And inclusion.

Segment 2: The Skimmers These folks opened emails. Sometimes clicked. Rarely replied. They were engaged, but not deeply.

Jenna shifted tone for them:

- Clearer subject lines

- Tighter formatting

- Skimmable design

She tested emails with fewer ideas but stronger framing: *"If you only read one thing today, let it be this."*

It worked. Replies increased. A few moved into the Warm Active segment.

Segment 3: The Dormant No opens in 45+ days. No replies. Still subscribed.

These readers needed contrast.

Jenna created a quarterly "pattern interrupt" email:

Subject: "We might need to break up."
Body:
"I'm clearing out the list this week. If you're still reading, click here. If not, I'll remove you—no hard feelings."

This reactivated a small group each time. More importantly, it preserved sender reputation and made space for new readers.

Segment 4: The Curious One-Offs These were new subscribers who clicked on the first or second email—but never again.

Jenna ran a small experiment. She sent them a personal-looking note:

"Hey, I saw you clicked on my teardown last week. Curious—was it what you expected?"

The response rate was low. But the replies she got were gold. They told her exactly where her tone, offer, or expectation-setting had gone off course.

From Broadcast to Threaded Conversations

Segmentation isn't just technical. It's relational.

Jenna began thinking of each segment as a conversation thread:

- The Warm Actives were continuing a dialogue

- The Skimmers were checking in

- The Dormant needed a reason to reengage

• The Curious One-Offs needed clarity

She didn't rewrite her whole calendar. She rewrote how she introduced and framed each message based on the reader's stage.

Dynamic Tone Matching

Using ESP automation, Jenna ran A/B tests with different voice tones for different segments:

• Warm Actives got conversational, off-the-cuff language

• Skimmers got direct, structured lines

• Dormants got emotional triggers and storytelling

The result: engagement increased across the board, especially replies. She wasn't guessing anymore. She was matching.

Building Segment-Specific Series Jenna built micro-sequences:

• A 3-email "you're new here" flow

• A 2-email "hey, you haven't opened in a while" message

• A 4-email "we see you clicking" series for repeat link-clickers

Each series referenced the subscriber's actions. This made every email feel like a continuation, not a reset.

The Ethical Side of Segmentation

Jenna was careful never to cross the line. She didn't say:

"We saw you clicked that PDF 6 times."

She said:

"Sounds like that inbox guide landed. Want the follow-up template too?"

Same action. Very different experience. Segmentation done right builds trust. Done wrong, it breaks it.

Manual Tagging and Light Automation Jenna didn't need a giant CRM or advanced AI. She started with a few rules:

• Tag all replies manually (e.g., "asked about deliverability")

• Use clicks to group by interest (e.g., "curious about CTAs")

• Move someone to Dormant after 45 days of no opens

Every week, she'd pull up her segments and write from that place. Not a campaign calendar. A reader profile.

Segmentation Is Empathy at Scale

Jenna's new strategy wasn't about hyper-personalization. It was about recognition.

When someone feels seen, they stay. When someone feels known, they engage.

Her open rate rose from 32% to 47%. Replies tripled. Unsubscribes dropped by 40%.

Not because her emails were better. Because they were better *matched*.

The Real Power of Behavior-Based Email Jenna now says:

"The most powerful line in any email is the one that shows you were paying attention."

She doesn't mean using {FirstName}. She means using phrases like:

"Since you downloaded the subject line doc..."

"If that last teardown got you thinking..."

"Looks like deliverability is top of mind for you."

These lines don't need to be sophisticated. They need to be true.

Section Recap: Speak to What They Do, Not Just Who They Are

Retention happens when readers feel understood. Segmentation is how you prove it.

In this section, we covered:

• Why behavior is a better segmenting signal than demographics

• How Jenna mapped her audience by actions and patterns

• What conversational tone-matching does for engagement

• Why light automation and tagging is more than enough

• How behavior-based messaging becomes the foundation of trust

In Section 3, we'll close out this chapter with long-term retention strategy—how to keep readers for months and years, how to reward loyalty, and how to gracefully exit relationships that have run their course.

Because attention is precious. And loyalty is earned one email at a time.

Chapter 6 - Section 3

Longevity Tactics:
How to Keep Your Readers
For Years

Jenna once believed that the true test of an email strategy was the launch. The open rate. The click-through. The conversion bump. But over time, she saw a deeper pattern emerge: the best-performing campaigns weren't driven by subject line hacks or fancy automations. They were powered by something quieter and longer-term.

Loyalty.

The subscribers who drove the most value didn't arrive through viral threads or flash campaigns. They stayed. They showed up every week. They became clients, referrers, collaborators. They didn't just consume her emails—they became part of the ecosystem.

And the turning point for Jenna came when she stopped focusing on acquisition and started asking a new question:

"How do I keep someone for a year?"

This section is about exactly that—how to build a list that doesn't just grow but compounds in value over time. Because your greatest marketing asset isn't just your message.

It's the people who never stop listening.

The Three Phases of Reader Loyalty

Jenna began thinking about retention not as a metric, but as a journey. Every long-term subscriber passed through three phases.

First came curiosity. This was the spark—usually triggered by a tweet, a podcast, a referral. It led to the first open. The first click.

Then came familiarity. This was where most readers got stuck. They liked her emails. They skimmed. They maybe clicked once or twice. But they weren't deeply invested yet. They hadn't made the shift from consumer to participant.

And finally, there was attachment. These readers weren't just engaged—they were loyal. They replied. They mentioned her in Slack channels. They forwarded emails to colleagues. They became part of the brand.

Jenna realized that each phase had different emotional needs.

Curiosity needed clarity. Familiarity needed rhythm. Attachment needed depth.

So she rebuilt her strategy to support all three.

From Curiosity to Familiarity: Making the Early Weeks Matter

Most churn happens in the first 30 days. Jenna had seen it. People would sign up, open once or twice, then vanish. She realized that the window for building momentum was brutally short.

She began optimizing her welcome experience like an onboarding flow. Not with a 10-part funnel, but with real intention.

The first email wasn't an intro. It was a story.

It said:

"You don't need another newsletter. But you might need better conversations. Here's why I send this."

It wasn't polished. It was personal. And that was the point.

The second email referenced the first. It reinforced identity: "If you're still here, you're my kind of reader." It offered a simple choice: reply or click. Start the loop.

Jenna learned that momentum was emotional. Once a reader opened three emails in a row, they were 4x more likely to stay long term.

So she designed her first five emails to be momentum engines. Not content. Moments.

Each one built on the last. Each one offered a piece of the bigger picture. Each one deepened the why.

She wasn't onboarding a subscriber. She was onboarding a belief system.

From Familiarity to Attachment: Building Deep Recognition

The challenge with mid-term readers was different. They knew her name. Her tone. They might even trust her.

But they hadn't yet connected emotionally.

Jenna realized that loyalty doesn't come from frequency. It comes from moments of resonance—when the reader feels that the email wasn't just smart, but meant for *them*.

So she built "recognition moments" into her flow.

She started referencing prior messages. She'd say, "Last month I wrote about how replies drive inbox placement. A few of you asked for proof. Here's the case study."

This made readers feel included. It showed her memory.

She also began naming her content. Not with big brand-y names, but with phrases her readers could reference.

She said, "This is the 'Empty Calendar' method."

Soon, people replied saying, "That calendar method? We used it. It worked."

Naming ideas gives readers language. Language builds identity. Identity creates attachment.

And in long-term retention, identity is the glue.

Creating Signature Series and Seasonal Content

People remember patterns. Jenna decided to give them one.

She created quarterly themes—each with a short sequence of 3-4 emails that built on each other.

Q1: Clean Your List
Q2: Engineer Replies
Q3: Deliverability Deep Dive
Q4: The Year-End Reengagement System

Each season had a rhythm. Each message was standalone, but when read together, they felt like a curriculum.

Readers knew what was coming. They looked forward to it. And they stuck around to see the arc unfold.

This gave her content structure and gave her readers reason to keep showing up.

She also ran one annual "State of the Inbox" piece—part data, part commentary, part invitation.

That email got more replies than any other.

Not because it was perfect. But because it felt timely. Shared. Real.

Personal Notes That Scale Emotionally, Not Logistically

Every few weeks, Jenna wrote what she called a "zero-agenda email."

It didn't sell. It didn't teach. It just shared.

Sometimes it was a mistake she made. Sometimes a client win. Sometimes just a late-night thought.

But always real. Always from her. Not the marketer version. The person.

And those emails got saved. Shared. Screenshot. They reminded readers: behind the list is a voice. Behind the voice is a human.

That's what makes a reader stay.

Not the next tactic. But the ongoing relationship.

Loyalty as a Two-Way Street

Jenna knew that some of her readers had been with her for years.

So she started giving back.

Every quarter, she sent a private email to her longest-tenured subscribers.

"You've been here 18 months. That means something to me. Here's something I don't share publicly."

Sometimes it was a doc. Sometimes a free session. Sometimes just a thank-you.

No conditions. No tracking.

She called these her "Loyalty Loops."

And they paid back in ways no funnel ever could.

The Graduation Email

Sometimes, retention means knowing when to let go.
Jenna created what she called the "Graduation Email."

If someone hadn't opened in 90 days, but had once been active, they got this:

Subject: "Let's part with gratitude."
Body:
"This isn't a breakup. Just a sendoff. You haven't opened in a while, and I don't want to take up space you didn't ask for. So unless you click here, I'll unsubscribe you—no guilt. Just gratitude."

People replied with kindness. With memories. With thanks.
Some reengaged. Some left.
Either way, it honored the relationship.
Because in great email marketing, relationships matter more than metrics.

Why Jenna's List Became a Moat

Two years after her retention shift, Jenna's list was smaller than some competitors. But it outperformed them in every metric.
Her open rates hovered near 50%. Her reply rates were consistently over 12%. Her unsubscribe rate was under 0.1%.
Her list *compounded*.
Not through hacks. But through habit. Through relevance. Through resonance. Through rhythm.
Because the best way to grow a list isn't just to add. It's to stop losing the ones who already cared.

Section Recap: Loyalty Is a System, Not a Fluke

Retention doesn't happen on accident. It's engineered.

Jenna learned that to keep subscribers long-term, she had to:

- Treat onboarding like a relationship, not a transaction

- Design seasonal arcs that give people a reason to stay

- Include recognition and identity-building moments in her flow

- Offer personal stories and behind-the-scenes notes to stay human

- Give loyalty its own reward

- Exit subscribers gracefully, not just silently

In Chapter 7, we'll turn to monetization—how to turn your list into revenue without breaking trust, pushing too hard, or ruining the careful relationship you've spent all this time building.

Because the real power of a retained list is what it lets you do next.

Chapter 7
Selling Without Burning:
Turning Trust Into Revenue

Section 1: Rethinking Monetization

The Email Sale That Doesn't Feel Like Selling

"Trust is built with consistency."
— Lincoln Chafee

J enna had a list that opened, clicked, and replied. She'd built trust, developed rituals, and created a system where her audience didn't just read—they looked forward to hearing from her. But now came the moment that makes most email marketers nervous:

Selling.

She'd seen what happens when people do it wrong. Flashy promotions. Endless discounts. A shift in tone so abrupt it breaks the reader's trust. And then—silence. People unsubscribe. Replies slow down. Revenue comes in, but reputation takes a hit.

Jenna didn't want to trade short-term revenue for long-term damage. So she asked a deeper question:

"How can I sell in a way that strengthens the relationship?"

The answer wasn't in tactics. It was in philosophy.

This section is about that philosophy—and the structure it led Jenna to use. Not a pitchfest. A conversation. One that made sales feel natural, even welcome. Because when trust is high, selling doesn't feel like pressure. It feels like service.

What Most Email Sales Get Wrong

Jenna reviewed dozens of campaigns—hers and others. The pattern was clear.

Most email promotions fail not because of bad offers, but because of emotional dissonance. The shift from value-driven to pitch-driven is too sharp. The reader feels it. It makes them flinch.

They think:

- "Oh, this is different."

- "They want something now."

- "I thought we were building something else."

It's not that people hate being sold to. It's that they hate feeling *misled*.

So Jenna built her monetization strategy on a simple rule: make the sale feel like the next step, not a new conversation.

Start the Sale Before You Pitch

Jenna's most successful sales didn't begin with a CTA. They began with a shift in attention.

She'd start planting seeds 2–3 emails before an offer:

• "I've been thinking a lot about what makes readers actually reply."

• "One of our consulting clients saw a 3x reply rate last month. I'll show you how we got there next week."

These weren't teasers. They were context-builders.

They framed the coming sale as part of the journey. A deepening, not a detour.

The Soft Frame: How Jenna Introduced Paid Offers

When it came time to pitch, Jenna used what she called the "soft frame."

She didn't lead with urgency or price. She led with clarity and alignment.

Example:

"I've spent the last 3 months working on something for people who want to write emails that actually get replies—not just clicks. If that's you, this might be worth a look."

Then she added:

"No pressure. I'll tell you what it is tomorrow. For now, just know it's built for folks who've been here a while."

That line—"for folks who've been here a while"—did more than any testimonial.
It reminded readers: this is for us. This is the thing we've been talking about. The natural next step.

The Launch Without the Fireworks

When Jenna finally launched her course, she didn't use a countdown clock. She used a short story.

She wrote:

"Three years ago, I sent an email that got 34 replies. I didn't know why it worked. So I started testing. This course is everything I learned since that day."

That story made the offer feel like a gift—not a transaction.

She followed with five simple emails:

1. The Origin — Why she made it

2. The Fit — Who it's for and who it's not

3. The Breakdown — What's inside

4. The Hesitation — Why she waited to release it

5. The Close — Final invite, no urgency, just clarity

Each email felt like an extension of her usual rhythm. Tone: same.

Structure: same. CTA: present, but never pushy.

And it worked.

Open rates stayed above 45%. Unsubscribes stayed under 0.3%. Sales exceeded her goal by 42%.

Most importantly—replies poured in. People said thank you. Not just for the offer. For how it felt.

The Invisible CTA

One of Jenna's favorite techniques was what she called the "invisible CTA."

Instead of a big button or bolded link, she wrote:

"If you're curious, I tucked the details here."

Or:

"Here's the page, if you're in that season."

This made the reader feel in control. It avoided the mental pressure of being "sold to."

She tested bold CTAs, image buttons, urgency timers. The invisible CTA performed best with her audience.

Because when trust is high, subtlety converts.

Pricing as Positioning

Jenna also rethought how she talked about price. Instead of anchoring value by comparison ("it's like the price of one coffee a day!"), she anchored value by outcome.

She said:

"If this gets you one high-reply email a month, it pays for itself in less than a

week."

She priced based on clarity, not affordability. She wanted her readers to invest, not react.

And for those who couldn't yet invest? She kept her free content as valuable as ever.

The message was clear: "Buy if you're ready. If not, stay. I'm still here."

Mini-Offers Between Big Campaigns

Not every monetization moment had to be a launch.

Jenna built small, context-based offers into her email flow:

• After a teardown email, she'd say:

"If you want 3 more examples like this, I put them in a PDF."

• After a reply-heavy thread, she'd write:

"Sounds like inbox placement's top of mind. This short workshop might help."

These were low-pressure, high-fit moments. And they converted 3x better than traditional promo sequences.

Because they felt like help, not hustle.

From Buyers to Ambassadors

Jenna's goal wasn't just revenue. It was loyalty.

So after someone bought, she didn't just send a receipt. She sent a thank-you email that said:

"This means a lot. If you liked it, tell me what worked. If you didn't, tell me why. Either way, thanks for trusting me."

She included a hidden bonus for buyers who replied. Not for engagement. For relationship.

Many of those buyers became advocates. They referred others. They stayed on the list. They bought again.

Because the sale wasn't the end. It was a beginning.

Section Recap: Sell Like You Talk

Email selling doesn't have to be slick. It has to be real.

In this section, we covered:

• Why trust collapses when the tone shifts too fast

• How Jenna built anticipation before her pitch

• What "soft framing" does for reader alignment

• How invisible CTAs and gentle pricing language keep readers engaged

• Why post-purchase communication drives retention

In Section 2, we'll go deeper into campaign architecture—how to build launch sequences that don't feel like launches, and how to sell with empathy, clarity, and pacing that matches your reader's trust level.

Because the most powerful sales don't interrupt the conversation. They continue it.

Chapter 7 - Section 2

Campaigns That Convert Without Pressure

Once Jenna learned how to introduce an offer without breaking the emotional thread of her emails, she realized she needed a structure that could hold the offer for more than one message. A full campaign. But one that didn't feel like a campaign.

She had seen the typical launch formula—scarcity, urgency, countdown timers, case studies, testimonials, bonuses, and the rest. And while it worked in some spaces, it didn't fit her audience. Her list wasn't driven by hype. It was driven by trust.

So she built a different kind of campaign architecture. One that didn't rely on pressure, gimmicks, or hard closes. Instead, it used emotional pacing, conversational continuity, and thoughtful timing to turn interest into investment.

This section breaks down that approach.

The Campaign as a Journey, Not a Pitch

Jenna began by throwing out the term "launch." She didn't want to "launch" at her list. She wanted to invite them into something.

So she started calling her sales campaigns "sequences." It was a small language shift, but it helped her stay grounded. She wasn't building funnels. She was building stories.

She decided each sales sequence should have three parts: alignment, offer, and decision. These weren't emails. They were phases.

Alignment was about reminding the reader who they were and what they believed. Offer was about introducing the path. Decision was about helping them choose.

That structure gave her freedom. She didn't need a script. She needed a progression.

Phase One: The Alignment Sequence

This began before anything was for sale. Jenna would write two or three emails designed to reconnect readers to the original pain or aspiration they had when they joined her list.

She didn't talk about her product. She talked about the gap.

For example, before opening the doors to her deliverability playbook, she sent an email called "The Quiet Cost of Being Ignored."

It wasn't a promo. It was a reflection.

She told a story about a time she spent weeks on an email that flopped. She talked about what that silence felt like. She then invited readers to reply if they'd experienced it too.

Dozens did.

Then she followed with another message: "Why Most Email Advice is 10 Years Outdated."

She didn't name names. She just named the frustration her readers already felt.

By the time she was ready to talk about her product, readers were already saying, "I hope you have something for this."

That's alignment.

Phase Two: The Offer Sequence

When Jenna introduced the offer, she didn't do it in one big sales email. She unfolded it slowly. Each message revealed a new piece.

Day one was the backstory: why she built it, what problem it solved. Day two was the structure: what's inside, how it works. Day three was the fit: who it's for and who it's not. Day four was the promise: what happens if you do it. Day five was the reminder: here if you need it.

Each email stood alone. But together, they built a rhythm.

None of them relied on hard sells. Each one felt like a chapter in a conversation.

What surprised Jenna most was the reply volume. Readers didn't just buy. They asked questions. They shared hesitations. They told her where they were stuck.

That told her she was doing it right.

Because good sales emails don't close. They open.

The Emotional Timing of a Sale

Jenna learned that the most powerful conversion driver wasn't urgency. It was timing.

Not calendar timing. Emotional timing.

She asked herself, "What is my reader going through this week? This quarter? This season?"

When she timed her offer with a moment of felt tension, it landed.

For example, she ran her inboxing playbook campaign in mid-January, when most email lists were rebounding from holiday fatigue. Her readers were already thinking about deliverability. Her offer became a solution, not a sales pitch.

She wasn't just selling. She was aligning with a moment.

The Middle Email — Where Sales Are Won

Most campaigns lose energy in the middle. Jenna made sure hers didn't.

Instead of repeating benefits or adding bonuses, she used the middle email for vulnerability.

She'd write something like:

"I almost didn't release this. I thought maybe it was too obvious. Maybe too small. But then someone told me they spent six months getting back into Primary because no one showed them this. That's why I hit send."

That email always performed.

Not because it was clever. But because it was honest.

It reminded readers that behind the offer was a human. Not a funnel. Not a launch. Just someone trying to help.

Anticipating Objections Before They're Asked

Jenna also wrote objection emails—but not the pushy kind.

She asked herself, "What are the three most honest reasons someone wouldn't buy this?"

Then she wrote an email for each one.

One was about time. She acknowledged the fear of not implementing. She offered a lite version.

Another was about overwhelm. She framed the offer as a toolkit, not a course. Something you could dip into, not complete.

The third was about distrust. She referenced past readers who said, "I've bought ten of these and never used them."

She replied:

"Same. That's why I built this differently. Here's how."

These weren't objections to overcome. They were hesitations to empathize with.

And they worked.

Because readers don't need you to be persuasive. They need you to be real.

Reader-Led Sales: The Reply Funnel

Sometimes Jenna wouldn't even launch publicly.

She'd send a quiet email:

"I made something for people who want better reply rates in 2024. I haven't shared it yet. Want a peek?"

Whoever replied got the offer.

No list-wide pitch. No countdowns. Just a hand-raise moment.

These micro-launches converted better per reader than any of her public campaigns.

Not because the offer was better. Because the reader invited it.

The Post-Sale Momentum Plan

After a sale, Jenna didn't disappear. She showed up.

She sent a thank-you note. A short voice memo. A surprise bonus.

Then, a week later, she'd send a non-sales email referencing the campaign.

"Thanks to everyone who joined the playbook last week. If you missed it, no worries. But
here's a tip from inside it you can use right now."

This kept momentum going. And kept non-buyers engaged.

Because the best sales campaign doesn't divide your list. It deepens your relationships—with buyers and browsers alike.

Designing Campaigns That Feel Like Conversations

Jenna now thinks of every campaign as a campfire.

She's not broadcasting. She's gathering.

The messages are like logs. Each one adds warmth. Adds clarity. Adds story.

Some people pull up a chair early. Some come closer near the end.

But no one feels pushed. No one feels tricked. No one feels like they're being funneled.

That's why her campaigns work.

Not because they're optimized. Because they're *inviting*.

Section Recap: Campaigns Built on Respect Convert Better

You don't need more pressure. You need more progression.

In this section, we covered:

• How Jenna structured her sales into three emotional phases: alignment, offer, decision

• Why emotional timing matters more than urgency

• How she used stories, questions, and quiet honesty to build momentum

• What the "middle email" can do to deepen trust

• How small reader-led sales outperform big launches

• Why post-sale communication keeps the list warm for next time

In Section 3, we'll cover offer design itself—how to build products and services that your list actually wants to buy, and how to use your emails to test, refine, and co-create your offers before you ever launch.

Chapter 7 - Section 3

The Offers Your Audience Actually Wants

When Jenna first started selling through email, she did what most people do—she built what she thought her audience needed, packaged it in a format she saw others using, and launched it with a mix of hope and hustle.

It worked… but only kind of. Her audience bought, but the offers felt heavy. Fulfillment took more time than expected. The feedback loop was weak. Something was off.

Then she realized the real leverage wasn't in the sales emails—it was in the offer design itself.

A great offer doesn't just convert. It creates momentum, satisfaction, and advocacy. And most importantly, it fits the emotional context of your audience: what they believe, what they're struggling with, how they want to grow, and how they like to engage.

This section is about how Jenna rebuilt her offers—not from data, but from conversation. Not from templates, but from need. It's a roadmap for creating products and services that sell themselves because they're shaped with, not just for, the reader.

Listening as Product Development

The first shift Jenna made was simple: she stopped guessing.

She used her inbox as a product lab. Every reply, every offhand comment, every hesitation was a signal.

When a reader asked, "Do you have a swipe file for this?" She wrote it down.

When another asked, "I've read your emails for months—do you coach?" She paid attention.

Her most successful products didn't come from brainstorming sessions. They came from inbox friction. The questions that showed up again and again.

She created a running note with these prompts:

• What are readers struggling with?

- What do they ask for directly?

- What do they hint at indirectly?

- What language do they use?

She called it her Demand File.

Once a quarter, she'd scan it. The patterns always pointed to the same truths:

- Her readers valued simplicity.

- They didn't want courses. They wanted clarity.

- They didn't trust tactics. They trusted tools.

That changed everything.

Co-Creation Over Assumption

Instead of disappearing into course creation, Jenna started involving her list in the offer design.

She'd send a short note:

"I'm building something to help with reengagement emails. If you had a magic wand, what would it include?"

The responses were gold. Some were emotional: "I just want to stop feeling ghosted." Others were tactical: "A few examples that actually worked would be great."

She used those words in her copy. She used those desires in her content.

When she released the product, readers recognized it. It sounded like them. It solved their version of the problem—not some abstract version dreamed up in a vacuum.

That's why it sold.

Because it didn't feel like a product. It felt like an answer.

Format Fit: Matching the Offer to the Audience

Jenna also stopped forcing her content into formats that didn't fit.

At first, she thought she had to sell courses. Everyone was doing it. But her audience didn't want 20 videos.

They wanted checklists. Swipe files. Templates. Scripts. Things they could copy, tweak, and use today.

So she created:

• A Google Doc with subject line tests

• A Notion template for reengagement flows

• A 3-email sequence with commentary

Each was low production. But high value.

And because they were easy to deliver, she could respond fast. Test fast. Improve fast.

Later, she layered on higher-ticket offers—like audits, consults, and strategy intensives. But those came after she had proof that her framework worked.

She didn't lead with scale. She led with fit.

Pricing for Confidence, Not Clicks

Jenna realized that most pricing advice was built around psychology tricks: charm pricing, scarcity, decoys.

But her readers were sensitive to manipulation. They didn't mind paying—but they wanted to feel respected.

So she shifted her pricing to reflect clarity.

Instead of:

"$97 today only!"

She wrote:

"This is $150. It's not cheap, but if it gets you back into the inbox, it's a rounding error."

And it worked.
Because pricing, like copy, is a mirror. If you price for trust, you attract people who trust.
Testing Offers Inside the Email

Sometimes Jenna didn't even build the product first. She floated the idea in a PS line:

"Thinking of putting together a mini playbook for reengaging cold subs. If that's useful, reply 'YES' and I'll prioritize it."

Thirty-five replies. She made the product that week. It sold out within 48 hours.

Other times, she would offer something live:

"Want me to review your email in a Loom video? $50 for the first five."

She didn't have a sales page. She didn't have a funnel. She had an idea. A test. And a reader.
That's enough.

Evolving Offers Based on Use, Not Spec

Once Jenna released a new offer, she didn't assume it was done.

She watched how people used it. She asked what they skipped. She noticed what they misunderstood.

And she iterated.

Her second version of a checklist became shorter. Her third version added an explainer video. Her fourth had space for reader notes.

These weren't new products. They were *refined* products.

That's why they kept selling. Because they kept improving.

The "Always Available" Dilemma

One of Jenna's early fears was that if her offers were always available, they'd lose urgency.

But she found the opposite to be true.

If the product was useful, and if the reader was ready, they bought.

So she started anchoring her messages around moments, not launches.

"Just ran a teardown with a client using this doc."

"Reply rates dropped this week—this might help."

By tying her offer to real-time needs, she created natural urgency. No timers. Just timing.

Creating a Product Stack That Reflects a Path

Eventually, Jenna created a light product ladder—not by forcing tiers, but by observing needs.

The path was simple:

1. Free checklist (trust)

2. Low-ticket templates (confidence)

3. Mini course or doc (skill)

4. Live training or audit (support)

5. High-ticket engagement (transformation)

Each step was optional. But each prepared the reader for the next.

Because good monetization isn't just about money. It's about momentum.

Why Jenna's Offers Keep Selling

Years into her email journey, Jenna's offer suite looked nothing like her original plan.

It wasn't flashy. It wasn't highly produced.

But it sold consistently. It got results. And her readers loved it.

Why?

Because it wasn't built for scale. It was built for fit.

Every email was part of the research. Every reply was part of the roadmap. Every offer was a reflection of what the reader had already told her they needed.

That's what makes it sustainable.

Because in the end, great email sales don't start with the pitch. They start with *listening*.

Section Recap: Build What They Already Want

In this section, we explored:

• How Jenna used conversation to shape her products

• Why co-creation builds resonance and trust

• What format fit means for offer delivery

• How pricing clarity increases buyer confidence

• Why reader-driven tests beat funnel-driven launches

• How to evolve products with actual use, not assumptions

In Chapter 8, we'll explore list protection—how to handle churn, clean your list without fear, and build sustainable growth without relying on constant addition.

Because your list isn't just a sales engine. It's an ecosystem. And healthy ecosystems need maintenance.

Chapter 8
Protect the Asset:
Maintaining List Health
and Sustainable Growth

Section 1: The Hidden Cost of a Bloated List

"Quality is more important than quantity. One home run is much better than two doubles."
— Steve Jobs

J enna had built a high-performing email list. Her subscribers opened, clicked, replied, and bought. But even in the middle of success, she knew something important: every list—no matter how well-built—starts to decay.

It doesn't happen all at once. It's slow. Silent. Invisible, until one day you notice your open rates slipping. Your replies dropping. The clicks that once felt effortless now require friction. And that's when most marketers panic.

They think, "I need to grow faster. I need to launch again. I need more leads."

But Jenna took a different approach.

She decided to protect what she'd already built.

This chapter is about list maintenance. Not just hygiene—but stewardship. Because a healthy list isn't just a marketing asset. It's a living system. And like any living system, it needs care, pruning, and protection.

Why Decay Happens (Even to Great Lists)

Email decay is inevitable. People change jobs. They lose interest. They sign up on a whim and forget. Their priorities shift. Their inbox habits evolve.

None of this is personal. But it affects everything.

Even Jenna—who had a thoughtful onboarding, consistent content, and high engagement—saw churn. Every week, a few more cold subscribers. A few more passive opens. A few more quiet unsubscribes.

But instead of chasing growth to outrun decay, she designed systems to *manage* it.

She shifted from list building to list *health*.

The Danger of Dead Weight

Inactive subscribers don't just take up space. They distort your data.

When a large portion of your list doesn't engage, you start making false assumptions:

• Subject lines aren't working

• Content is weak

• Deliverability is broken

But often, the issue isn't the email. It's the reader.

When Jenna analyzed her metrics, she saw a consistent pattern: her active segment opened at 48% and replied at 9%. Her inactive segment opened at 2% and never replied.

And yet—she had been sending them the same messages.

That's when she realized: keeping them wasn't just neutral. It was *harmful*.

Dead weight hurt her sender reputation. It pulled down her averages. And worst of all, it distracted her from writing for the people who still cared.

So she made the hard call: clean the list.

Reframing List Cleaning as Service

At first, the idea of removing subscribers felt like loss.

Jenna had worked hard to build her list. Every address represented time, effort, and investment. Deleting them felt counterintuitive—especially when conventional wisdom says more is more.

But then she reframed the act. It wasn't about subtraction. It was about respect.

Respect for the reader, who shouldn't be forced to receive content they no longer want. Respect for the active subscribers, who deserve higher deliverability and better inbox placement. Respect for herself, so she could write with clarity and confidence.

From that lens, pruning became service.

How Jenna Designed Her Cleaning Process

She started with a few clear rules:

1. If a subscriber hadn't opened or clicked in 60 days, they were flagged.

2. If they hadn't engaged in 90, they were moved to a dormant segment.

3. Every quarter, she ran a re-engagement campaign to that segment.

4. If they didn't respond to that campaign, they were removed.

No drama. No emotion. Just stewardship. The re-engagement campaign was short. Three emails.

• The first: "Still interested?"

• The second: "I'll be removing inactive folks next week."

• The third: "Final call—stay or go."

Each was written with kindness, not guilt.
Subscribers who clicked or replied were reactivated. The rest were quietly unsubscribed.
The result? A smaller list. But a sharper one.

The Deliverability Boost That Followed

Within two weeks of her first full list clean, Jenna saw immediate improvement:

• Open rates increased from 35% to 47%

• Replies rose by 22%

• Her spam complaints dropped to basically zero

• Her average placement in Gmail improved

She wasn't just improving metrics. She was regaining trust—from her readers, and from the algorithms.

This became her new rule:

"If I wouldn't email this person manually, they shouldn't be on the list."

Handling Edge Cases with Care

Jenna didn't apply rules blindly. She gave herself discretion.

Some subscribers rarely clicked, but replied often. Some opened inconsistently but forwarded regularly.

She looked at *patterns*, not just data points.

A reader might not open for 60 days—then suddenly reply with, "This one really hit."

So she gave space for nuance.

That's why she used tags instead of deletions. That way, she could re-add people manually if they reached out.

She also started tracking reader histories—not just engagement, but tenure.

A 2-year reader with low activity got more grace than a 2-week subscriber with none.

Because retention isn't just numbers. It's relationships.

Why Fewer Subscribers Made Her Write Better

When Jenna's list was bloated, she wrote defensively. She tried to keep everyone happy. She diluted her message to avoid churn.

But after the clean?

She wrote sharper. Clearer. More herself.

Because she wasn't speaking to ghosts. She was speaking to real readers who showed up. Who cared. Who replied.

That confidence changed her tone. Her pacing. Her stories.

Her emails got better—not because her skills improved, but because her audience did.

Turning Clean-Up Into a Ritual

Now, Jenna doesn't see cleaning as a reaction. She sees it as maintenance.

Every quarter, she blocks one day for a full audit:

- Export engagement reports

- Sort by last open and click

- Review replies and manual notes

- Move dormant subscribers into suppression

She calls it "The Garden Day."

Because that's what her list is: a garden. Something living. Something worth tending.

Section Recap: Prune to Thrive

You don't grow a powerful list by keeping everyone. You grow it by keeping the right ones.

In this section, we covered:

- Why decay is inevitable, but manageable

• How inactive readers hurt engagement, clarity, and confidence

• Jenna's simple process for flagging, segmenting, and removing cold subscribers

• The emotional reframing that made pruning feel like service

• Why fewer readers made her emails stronger

• How maintenance becomes momentum

In Section 2, we'll go deeper into building a system for sustainable growth—how to balance retention and acquisition, how to pace your outreach, and how to protect your sender reputation while still expanding your reach.

Because growth isn't just about more. It's about *health*.

Chapter 8 - Section 2

Systems That Grow Without Compromising Trust

After Jenna learned how to prune her list for health, she faced the other side of the retention equation: growth. It's easy to think of growth as the counterbalance to list decay. For every reader lost, add another. Maintain the number. Keep the chart rising.

But that mindset leads to a dangerous trap: valuing quantity over quality.

The real goal isn't just to grow. It's to grow with intention. Sustainably. In a way that preserves trust, maintains tone, and improves—not erodes—your signal strength.

That's the challenge Jenna took on: how to grow without compromising the integrity she worked so hard to build.

She started by replacing the word "growth" with a better one: *alignment.*

Because the best subscribers aren't found. They're *aligned.*

What Sustainable Growth Actually Means

Most marketers chase growth as a reaction. Open rates dip? Buy ads. Launch isn't converting? Build a bigger list. Metrics flatline? Try a giveaway.

But sustainable growth flips the logic. It's proactive. Strategic. Rooted in audience quality, not marketing anxiety.

Jenna broke it down like this; growth is sustainable when:

• New subscribers are more likely to engage than churn

• Acquisition systems don't damage sender reputation

• Every entry point mirrors the experience inside the emails

• Volume never overrides voice

This was her new bar.

Any growth strategy that met those standards was in. Everything else—even if it worked on paper—was out.

Designing Entry Points That Prime, Not Just Capture

Jenna revisited her opt-in flow.

She asked, "What would it look like to make every step of the subscriber journey reflect the same voice, tone, and standards as my emails?"

That meant changing everything:

• Her landing pages became conversational instead of optimized.

• Her CTAs shifted from urgency to alignment.

• Her confirmation email felt like a letter, not an automation.

Instead of "Join the newsletter," it was:

"If you like simple, plain-text, no-fluff ideas about writing emails people actually reply to, I write a few each week. If that sounds useful, sign up. If not, no worries."

This created a powerful filter.
Fewer subscribers signed up. But the ones who did? They stayed.

Pacing Acquisition to Match Attention

Jenna noticed that her best email seasons came when growth was steady—not spiky.

Big list spikes from podcast interviews or paid traffic often led to unstable metrics. Engagement dipped. Replies scattered. She lost her sense of the room.

So she created what she called "reader tempo."

She asked: How many new voices can I welcome before I lose the rhythm with my current ones?

She landed on a simple rule: no more than 10% of her total list should be brand-new in a 30-day period.

This kept her content relevant. It let her onboard new readers without alienating longtime subscribers.

And it gave her room to nurture before she asked for anything.

The Welcome Experience That Actually Works

Most onboarding flows are optimized for automation, not emotion.

Jenna reversed that.

Her welcome sequence wasn't a funnel. It was a trust-builder.

First email: her story. Not the resume version. The "why I write this list" version.

Second email: a favorite framework—with a question.

Third email: a case study, written like a conversation.

Fourth email: a quiet ask—"What brought you here?"

This sequence wasn't about conversion. It was about calibration.

Every new subscriber walked away knowing:

- Her tone

- Her standards

- Her worldview

- Her expectations

That reduced churn. Increased reply rate. And made every sales campaign smoother.

Because trust wasn't built during the pitch. It was built during the hello.

Avoiding the Viral Growth Trap

Jenna experimented with growth tactics. She tried contests. Giveaways. Co-branded lead magnets. Group bundles.

The results looked great on spreadsheets. Thousands of new subscribers in days.

But a month later? Silence. Unsubs. Complaints. Ghosts.

The issue wasn't the campaign. It was *incongruence*.

These subscribers didn't know her voice. They hadn't chosen her. They didn't arrive through resonance.

So she made a new rule: no growth without context.

She wouldn't run a campaign unless she had space to *introduce herself first*. That meant partnerships came with guest emails. Ads pointed to long-form content. Every list boost had a pre-frame.

That one shift changed everything.

The subscribers who stayed felt like they *belonged*.

Growth Channels That Don't Break Deliverability

Every list spike carries a risk: deliverability.

Jenna knew that if too many cold subscribers ignored her first few emails, her inbox placement would suffer.

So she created a "warming layer."

Every new subscriber was segmented. Before they received her normal broadcasts, they got a light onboarding sequence.

If they opened at least one of the first three emails, they graduated. If not, they were tagged as cold.

Those cold subs? She paused them. Sometimes forever.

This protected her core list. And preserved her sender reputation.

Because not everyone deserves access.

Why Jenna Rejected Always-On Acquisition

It's tempting to leave ads running. To keep a steady stream of traffic. To automate the top of the funnel forever.

But Jenna saw what happened when she did:

• Less attention to onboarding

• More time spent fixing engagement dips

• Declining energy in her writing

So she replaced "always on" with "always ready."
When she had capacity—emotional, operational, and strategic—she opened a growth window. A campaign. A partnership.
Then she paused. Let the dust settle. Integrated new readers.
Growth became seasonal. Not sporadic. Not passive. Not infinite.
Just *right-sized*.

Creating a Growth Loop That Feeds Itself

Eventually, Jenna stopped thinking of growth as traffic. She saw it as trust.

Every great email created three paths:

1. Deeper belief (retention)

2. Stronger resonance (engagement)

3. Increased word of mouth (referrals)

So she optimized for the third.

At the end of her emails, she added a simple line:

"If you know someone who writes email and hates most email advice, forward this. They can sign up here."

It was soft. Untracked. But powerful.

Soon, her best subscribers came not from ads—but from other subscribers.

That's when she knew her growth system was working.

Because when readers recruit readers, growth compounds.

Protecting the Reader Experience During Growth

Every time Jenna added new people to her list, she asked:

• Does this change my tone?

• Do I feel like I'm writing to a crowd or a person?

• Would this message land the same for a day-one reader and a day-1000 reader?

If the answer was no, she slowed down.

Because no growth is worth losing your voice.

Your list is not a number. It's a conversation.

And you can't talk meaningfully if you don't know who you're talking to.

Jenna's Quarterly Growth Checklist

Every quarter, Jenna audited her growth system:

• Where are new subs coming from?

• Which channel has the highest retention?

- Which has the lowest?

- Is onboarding matching expectations?

- Am I growing faster than I can maintain?

She treated growth like a garden. Each seed mattered. Each plant needed water.

And anything that crowded the space—was removed.

Section Recap: Growth That Strengthens, Not Stretches

Growth isn't just about adding people. It's about adding the right people, at the right pace, in a way that protects what you've built.

In this section, we explored:

- How Jenna designed entry points that pre-aligned subscribers

- Why onboarding is the real growth lever

- How to avoid viral tactics that degrade trust

- What pacing does for reader experience and deliverability

- Why referrals outperform most acquisition tactics

In Section 3, we'll explore the metrics that matter—the ones that actually reflect list health, reader behavior, and long-term business impact. Not vanity stats. Not dashboard noise. Just the signals that tell the truth.

Because you can't grow—or protect—what you don't understand.

Chapter 8 - Section 3

The Metrics That
Actually Matter

A t every step of her email journey, Jenna had used data to guide her decisions. But in the early days, she realized something critical: most of the metrics everyone focused on were either misleading, misused, or meaningless.

Everyone talked about open rates, list size, click-through rates. These numbers were easy to grab, easy to chart, easy to chase. But Jenna saw firsthand how they led marketers to the wrong conclusions —and, worse, the wrong strategies.

She knew she needed a different lens. A better way to measure not just movement, but meaning. Because if email is about trust, then your metrics should measure relationships—not just activity.

This section explores how Jenna redefined success in her email marketing. What she tracked. What she ignored. And how that shift gave her clarity, confidence, and long-term results.

The Problem With Conventional Metrics

Jenna began with a simple realization: open rates lie.

They can be inflated by bots. Suppressed by privacy settings. Distorted by Gmail promotions. Worse, they don't reflect *engagement*— only access.

Click rates? Slightly better, but also incomplete. Many of her best emails didn't include links. Others invited replies. And sometimes, readers would forward emails or take action offline. None of that showed up on her dashboard.

So she stopped chasing opens and clicks as primary goals. She used them as indicators—not KPIs.

She started asking better questions:

- Are my readers opening consistently over time?

- Are they replying?

- Are they referencing past emails in their responses?

• Are they forwarding?

• Are they buying?

That shift in focus changed everything.

The Core Metric: Response Rate Over Time

Jenna realized that one of the clearest signs of a healthy list was not just who opened—but who *replied*.

Replies were unmissable. Real. Human. They couldn't be faked or gamed.

More importantly, they built deliverability. They started conversations. They made her feel like her writing mattered.

She began tracking what she called "reply rate decay": the percentage of new subscribers who replied at least once in their first 30, 60, and 90 days.

That gave her real insight.

If that number dropped, it meant her onboarding was weak—or her new acquisition source was misaligned.

If it rose, she knew she was attracting and resonating with the right people.

She didn't need to obsess over it. She just needed to watch the trend.

Retention as the Real North Star

The longer someone stayed on her list, the more likely they were to:

• Open

• Engage

• Buy

• Refer

Jenna treated retention as her primary growth metric. Not just "still subscribed," but still *engaged*.

She measured what she called "active lifespan": how long the average subscriber opened or replied to at least 50% of her emails.

It wasn't a stat her email software gave her automatically. She had to dig for it—export data, run filters, build her own report.

But it told her what no dashboard ever could: how long her writing was actually holding attention.

That number helped her forecast future revenue, plan content rhythms, and gauge emotional resonance.

And it gave her one more reason to prune her list regularly. Because subscribers who didn't contribute to that metric were just noise.

List Quality Score (LQS)

Eventually, Jenna built her own metric. She called it the List Quality Score.

It was simple: Number of active, engaged subscribers ÷ Total list size

It wasn't perfect. But it gave her a quick way to ask: Is my list *healthy*?

A high LQS meant she was sending to people who cared. A low LQS meant she was bloated, off track, or attracting the wrong readers.

She aimed for a score above 60%. Anything below 40% triggered a clean-up.

Again, the number itself wasn't the point. The point was mindset.

Jenna stopped trying to impress herself with size. She focused on strength.

The Email Health Snapshot

Once a month, Jenna did a pulse check. She opened her ESP, exported her last 30 days of data, and reviewed the following:

- Total sends

- Opens (and trends)

- Clicks (if applicable)

- Replies

- Forward rates

- New subscribers

- Unsubscribes

- Spam complaints

She asked herself:

- What's changing?

- Where's the drop-off?

- What's working unusually well?

Sometimes she found surprises. Like the fact that her best reply email had no link. Or that her new opt-in page converted worse, but produced higher long-term retention.

Those insights led to changes. But more importantly, they gave her control. She didn't fear the numbers anymore. She used them.

Reader Signals Beyond the Metrics

Not everything Jenna measured lived in the ESP.

She tracked:

- Which emails got quoted on social

- Which ones were mentioned in replies months later

- Which messages drove unexpected referrals

- Which lines people copied and pasted

These weren't metrics. They were signals.

She kept a folder of favorite replies. She screenshotted tweets and DMs that referenced her writing. She tagged patterns: ideas that landed, phrases that stuck.

That archive became her compass. When she felt unsure of what to write, she reread it. When she planned a launch, she used it for language. When she doubted her path, she leaned on it.

Because sometimes, the most important metric is: "Did this matter to someone?"

Email Metrics That Don't Matter (Much)

Jenna also made peace with the data she could safely ignore.

She stopped obsessing over:

- Time of open (too noisy)

- Device split (irrelevant to her plain-text style)

- A/B test micro-wins (she cared more about the long arc)

She realized that most email tools are built for marketers chasing volume, not relationships.

Her job wasn't to optimize for dashboard wins. It was to stay close to her people.

Using Metrics to Improve, Not Validate

Early on, Jenna used stats to validate her work. A high open rate made her feel good. A low reply rate made her anxious.

Now, she used data differently.

She didn't take any single number too seriously. She didn't tie her worth to the metrics.

Instead, she looked for patterns. Used numbers to ask questions. Treated analytics like a conversation.

That's why her work got better. Because she wasn't reacting to numbers. She was reflecting with them.

How She Shared Metrics With Her Team and Partners

As Jenna's business grew, she brought on collaborators—designers, copywriters, backend support.

Instead of sending dashboards, she gave them stories:

- "This email landed. Here's why I think it worked."

- "This one flopped. Let's study the tone."

- "Our new readers aren't replying. Let's fix onboarding."

The numbers were context. But the conversation was always about people.

That changed how her team operated. They weren't working for clicks. They were working for *connection*.

Using Data to Say Goodbye

Sometimes, metrics tell you when to stop.

When a reader hadn't opened or replied in 6+ months. When a sequence underperformed three cycles in a row. When a format once loved now felt stale.

Jenna used those moments to clean. To revise. To rest.

She didn't resist the truth the data showed. She welcomed it.

Because in email, endings are as important as beginnings.

Section Recap: Track What Moves the Relationship

Email metrics only matter if they help you write better. Serve deeper. Connect more.

In this section, we explored:

- Why conventional metrics mislead—and what to track instead

- How Jenna used replies and retention as core indicators

- What her List Quality Score told her about focus

- How signals outside the inbox informed her direction

- Why healthy lists aren't measured in opens, but in outcomes

In Chapter 9, we'll wrap it all up—how to future-proof your email practice, continue evolving, and stay relevant in a world where platforms shift, tools change, and inboxes get noisier by the day.

Because your greatest asset isn't just the list. It's your voice. And the relationships it builds, one message at a time.

Chapter 9

Stay in the Game:

Future-Proofing Your

Email Strategy

Section 1: Adapting Without Losing Yourself

"The only thing that is constant is change."
— Heraclitus

J enna never set out to be an email marketer. She was a writer, first and always. Her earliest messages were scrappy, honest, and personal. She didn't think about frameworks or funnels. She thought about people. About what might help. What might resonate. What might be worth five minutes in a stranger's inbox.

And it worked.

Her list grew. Her voice sharpened. Her confidence deepened. But as her success expanded, something else crept in: pressure.

She felt it everywhere—in the way her ESP pushed new automation tools, in the advice from marketing podcasts urging AI integration, in the client requests asking for video embeds, gamification, and chatbot integrations.

Suddenly, the landscape felt faster. More technical. Less human.

The same inbox that had once been a place of warmth and clarity was now filled with noise, innovation, and complexity.

And for the first time in a long time, Jenna asked herself: "Can I still do this my way?"

This chapter is about the long game. It's about how to adapt, evolve, and stay relevant—without losing your center.

Because email, like everything else, will change. But your voice can stay steady.

The Myth of Reinvention

Jenna used to believe that the best way to stay ahead was to constantly reinvent. New formats. New tools. New tones.

But each time she tried something radically different—an embedded video, a redesign, an AI-generated campaign—she felt a strange distance in her writing.

The engagement dipped. Replies grew colder. Her emails were still "good," but they didn't feel *true*.

And her readers felt it too.

One longtime subscriber replied: "I liked this. But it didn't sound like you."

That line hit hard.

So she stopped chasing reinvention. She started chasing *reconnection*.

Because the people who subscribed weren't asking for new tricks. They were asking for more of her.

Staying Simple in a Complicated Ecosystem

The email world evolved fast.

New deliverability protocols. New privacy updates. New competition from messaging platforms, community spaces, social DMs.

It was easy to feel behind.

But Jenna chose a different response: she simplified.

She doubled down on plain-text. On clear CTAs. On voice-first writing.

She tested other formats occasionally. But her core remained the same: simple, resonant, intentional.

And in a world full of noise, that *became* her edge.

Readers emailed her saying, "Yours is the only one I still open."

Not because she shouted louder. But because she stayed herself.

Evolving Inside the Frame

Staying consistent didn't mean staying static.

Jenna evolved. Her ideas sharpened. Her strategies grew. Her audience matured.

But she evolved *inside* the frame.

Her voice stayed curious, thoughtful, direct. Her structure stayed flexible, but familiar. Her frequency remained steady.

Instead of overhauling her brand every quarter, she let her body of work speak for itself.

She built a pattern library of ideas that kept showing up. She iterated on old topics with new insights. She revisited popular threads, adding depth.

The goal wasn't to always surprise. The goal was to deepen.

Navigating the Tech Landscape Without Getting Lost

Every month, there was a new tool. A new AI plugin. A new email analytics platform. A new visual builder.

At first, Jenna felt like she had to try everything. But the mental overhead piled up. Her writing slowed. Her sense of clarity eroded.

So she created a personal rule: No new tool unless it removes friction.

If it didn't make her process easier, faster, or more joyful—it didn't make the cut.

She kept her stack minimal:

• One ESP she trusted

• A writing app she loved

• A tag system she understood

She let go of bells and whistles. And reclaimed her momentum.

Balancing Automation With Authenticity

Jenna didn't resist automation. But she used it carefully.

She wrote every onboarding email herself. Every campaign. Every reply-worthy prompt.

Yes, she scheduled. Yes, she tagged. But she never outsourced voice.

When readers replied, they got her—or someone trained to write like her. Not a bot.

That built intimacy. And intimacy built loyalty.

As AI tools got better, she experimented. Let them draft outlines. Suggest subject lines. But the heart always came from her.

Because the long game in email isn't automation. It's *affection*.

Responding to Reader Behavior Without Losing Control

As her list grew, patterns emerged. Readers responded more to teardowns. Less to reflections. More to tactical advice. Less to storytelling.

It was tempting to chase what worked. To optimize for what got the most clicks.

But Jenna remembered: this list didn't start with tactics. It started with trust.

So she created a content rhythm that included both:

• High-value, high-performance content to deliver clear wins

• Low-performing but high-resonance content to keep her grounded

She didn't write *for* the algorithm. She wrote with it in mind.
A partnership. Not a sacrifice.

Making Peace With Platform Change

Jenna had seen peers panic when Apple rolled out Mail Privacy Protection. Or when Gmail adjusted promotions tab filters. Or when new competitors popped up in the creator economy.

But she reminded herself:

Technology will always shift. Trust endures.

So she kept her focus on the core.

Writing that made people feel seen. Topics that actually solved problems. CTAs that invited—not demanded—action.

She updated her headers. Optimized her deliverability. Cleaned her list.

But she didn't let fear dictate her direction.

Because every time a tool changed, her voice stayed the same.

And that was her moat.

Mentoring the Next Generation of Email Writers

Eventually, Jenna became a mentor. She taught others how to build with voice. How to stay centered. How to grow a list without losing yourself.

Her advice was simple:

• Write every email like you're talking to a person who's about to unsubscribe or become your biggest fan.

• Don't chase clever. Chase clarity.

• Trust takes longer to build than traffic.

She watched her students build beautiful, honest, profitable lists. And she saw herself in them.

That gave her energy to keep going. Not just for her list—but for the community around it.

Redefining Success One Year at a Time

Each January, Jenna asked the same question:

"What do I want this list to feel like this year?"

Not "how much should I grow?" or "what will I sell?" But feel.

She picked a theme:

Year 1: Trust

Year 2: Rhythm

Year 3: Depth

Year 4: Conversation

Each theme shaped her writing. Her strategy. Her offers.
It helped her adapt with direction. And grounded her in purpose.
Because when email has a purpose, it survives change.

Why Her List Still Works

Years in, Jenna's list still worked. Not because she had the best tech. Not because she had the biggest numbers.

But because she had:

• A steady voice

• A deep well of trust

• A willingness to adapt without contorting

Her emails didn't scream. They invited.
They didn't chase hacks. They created homes.
And that made all the difference.

Section Recap: Change What You Must, Protect What You Can

To stay relevant in a changing landscape, Jenna:

• Focused on simplicity as her strategic edge

- Let go of reinvention and leaned into refinement

- Used tools to support—not replace—her voice

- Adapted content rhythms without losing tone

- Set emotional themes to guide each year

In Section 2, we'll look at specific frameworks Jenna used to maintain momentum over time.

Because evolution isn't just about survival—it's about sustainable growth, clarity of direction, and a list that grows with you—not away from you.

Chapter 9 - Section 2

Frameworks for Long-Term

Momentum

For all her success, Jenna knew the hardest part of running a list wasn't starting it. It was sustaining it. Starting is thrilling. Your list is small, every reply feels like a milestone, every new subscriber a spark. But after the rush of launch and the novelty of those first few months, something shifts.

The inbox becomes routine. The engagement settles. And if you're not careful, the voice that once felt electric starts to dull.

Jenna refused to let that happen.

So she created systems—frameworks not just for sending emails, but for staying in the game. These weren't rigid calendars or impersonal automation flows. They were practices. Rhythms. Creative scaffolding that kept her moving, without burning out or losing touch.

Because if your email list is an asset, you can't just write to it. You have to feed it, study it, protect it, and most of all—sustain it.

This section dives into the core frameworks Jenna used to build a long-term practice that didn't just work—but endured.

The Content Compass: A Simple Map for Staying on Message

Early on, Jenna created what she called her "content compass."

It was a four-quadrant framework. Each quadrant represented a type of message she knew her readers needed:

1. Personal stories that built emotional connection

2. Tactical how-to emails that delivered fast wins

3. Opinion pieces that established authority and earned shares

4. Behind-the-scenes messages that deepened intimacy and trust

Rather than plan content linearly, she rotated through the quadrants.

If she'd sent a tactical teardown one week, she'd follow it with a story. If she got heavy with opinion, she'd lighten it with a casual note about what she was experimenting with.

This rhythm helped her avoid content fatigue. It kept her voice fresh, her ideas balanced, and her readers engaged across different interest types.

She didn't overthink it. No color-coded charts. Just a sticky note on her monitor: *Connect. Teach. Provoke. Share.*

That little reminder became her roadmap.

The Feedback Loop: Turning Replies Into Direction

Momentum doesn't come from broadcasting. It comes from responding.

Jenna turned her inbox into an ongoing focus group. Every reply was an insight. Every question a breadcrumb. Over time, she noticed patterns.

She saw the same phrases surface again and again—"I feel stuck," "No one replies," "It's like shouting into the void."

Those weren't just pain points. They were cues.

So she built a habit. Every Friday, she'd spend an hour rereading replies. Highlighting language. Copying phrases. Jotting down themes.

From this she created:

• Idea lists for future emails

• Phrases to use in subject lines and CTAs

• Frameworks based on real reader language

That's how she stayed aligned. Not by guessing. By listening.
Even when her list scaled, this ritual stayed sacred.
Because direction doesn't come from analytics alone. It comes from attention.

The Pulse Week: Re-centering After Chaos

Not every season is stable. Sometimes launches drain you. Sometimes growth spikes throw off your rhythm. Sometimes life just gets messy.

Jenna built what she called "Pulse Week" for those moments.

Pulse Week was a return to the roots. One week a quarter, she skipped all tactics. She didn't pitch. Didn't test. Didn't follow any template.

She sent five emails. Plain, short, human. Each one answered one of these questions:

- What have I learned?

- What am I questioning?

- What am I afraid of?

- What surprised me?

- What do I want for you?

The point wasn't performance. It was presence.

These emails often got the most heartfelt replies. The most forwards. The most unsubscribes, too—but the right kind.

Pulse Week realigned her list. Re-established tone. It reminded her readers—and herself—what the list was for.

The Mid-Year Review: Your List as a Mirror

In July, Jenna ran a simple self-audit.

She asked:

- What emails got replies I still remember?

- Which ones felt flat, even if they "performed"?

- What did I love writing?

- What did I dread?

- Where am I holding back?

Then she'd open her archive. Read from January to June. Notice her voice.

She looked for drift—subtle tone changes, shifts in audience energy, fatigue creeping in.

If something felt off, she didn't blame herself. She just adjusted.

Sometimes she re-centered her themes. Other times, she added space. Occasionally, she pivoted completely.

The point wasn't to fix what wasn't broken. The point was to notice what wanted to evolve.

Your list isn't just a channel. It's a mirror. If it starts to feel off, chances are—you're off.

The mid-year review helped her course-correct before burnout took hold.

The Re-Onboarding Flow: Welcoming Yourself Back

There were seasons when Jenna stepped back. A health issue. A move. A business pivot.

Each time, the return was awkward. The temptation was to apologize, overexplain, or pretend nothing happened.

Instead, she created a "re-onboarding flow." Three simple emails:

1. A real update—what happened, where she is

2. A reflection—what the pause taught her

3. A re-commitment—what to expect going forward

These weren't just for the reader. They were for her.

They re-established rhythm. They re-anchored tone. They gave her permission to show up imperfectly.

Momentum isn't about never stopping. It's about knowing how to start again.

The Forever Folder: Remembering the Wins

Some weeks, the numbers felt low. The replies thin. The writing labored.

In those moments, Jenna opened her Forever Folder.

It was a digital archive of the best replies she'd ever received. Messages from readers who said:

- "I've saved every one of your emails."

- "This line stopped me mid-scroll."

- "I've never replied to a newsletter before, but…"

These were reminders. Of impact. Of resonance. Of why the work mattered.

She didn't read them to inflate her ego. She read them to refuel her heart.

The game of email is long. You need reminders that it's *worth* staying in.

The Offer Timeline: Selling Without Surprising

Momentum wasn't just about content. It was about pacing offers.

Jenna mapped her sales year in January—not because she loved planning, but because she knew surprise pitches broke trust.

She kept it loose:

- Q1: A new toolkit

- Q2: A cohort offer

- Q3: Quiet season, no pitch

- Q4: End-of-year teardown

Each season had a tone. And readers felt it.
This helped her space content. Set expectations. Avoid burnout.
Offers didn't feel like detours. They felt like milestones.
That made sales easier. And writing lighter.

Why These Frameworks Worked

Jenna's momentum didn't come from a calendar. It came from honoring her voice. Protecting her energy. Staying close to her audience.

The frameworks gave her just enough structure to keep going. But never so much she lost herself.

They reminded her:

- This is a practice.

- This is a relationship.

- This is yours.

And when you treat your list like something you belong to—not something you manage—you last.

Section Recap: Structure That Serves You

Jenna's long-term success wasn't about hacks or hustle. It was about:

- Building a flexible content map

- Turning replies into a compass

- Pausing regularly to pulse-check tone and energy

- Re-onboarding herself after breaks

- Holding a record of resonance

- Pacing her year to match her capacity

In Section 3, we'll close the book with the mindset shift that sustains everything: treating your email list not as an audience—but as a community.

Because the difference between a reader and a fan is how you see them. And how you let them see you.

Chapter 9 - Section 3

Turning a List
Into a Community

For a long time, Jenna thought her email list was a broadcast channel—a place to share ideas, build trust, offer help, and occasionally sell. That belief served her well. She respected her readers. She showed up consistently. She treated the list as a relationship.

But something changed the year she launched her most vulnerable product. It was a simple idea: a workshop series on how to write emotionally resonant emails. There was no big funnel. No affiliate plan. Just a note to her list, asking if they were interested.

What happened next wasn't just sales. It was *movement*.

Readers replied. They shared. They brought their colleagues. A few people offered to help promote without being asked. Someone built a Notion tracker of the series takeaways and posted it in a private Slack group. Another reader offered to translate the notes into Spanish for their own team.

It was in that moment Jenna realized: this wasn't just a list. It was a *community*.

Not in the traditional sense—there was no Facebook group, no portal. But there was connection. Shared identity. Shared values. Readers were talking to each other, not just Jenna.

That shift changed how she wrote. How she led. And how she saw her own work.

This section explores how Jenna moved from list to community. Not by building a membership site or Discord channel, but by deepening belonging and co-creation. Because when your readers feel seen—and when they see each other—your list becomes more than a marketing tool. It becomes a home.

Understanding the Difference

A list is one-to-many. A community is many-to-many.

On a list, readers receive. In a community, they *respond*. Share. Extend.

It's not about interactivity alone. It's about identity.

Jenna began to realize that her best readers didn't just like her content. They saw themselves *in it*.

They quoted her in team meetings. They used her phrases in their own copy. They saw her list not as a subscription—but as a place.

That insight led her to ask: what makes people feel like they belong?

Naming the Room

Jenna noticed something small but powerful. When she called her readers "you all," or "subscribers," her emails felt generic. But when she gave them a shared identity—"this crew," "the reply-first crowd," "fellow email nerds"—everything changed.

The shift was subtle. But human brains crave identity. We want to be part of something. We want our email habits, our style, our tone to *mean* something.

So Jenna gave them a name.

Not a brand. A banner.

She started using phrases like:

• "If you're someone who believes email is a conversation, not a campaign, you're home here."

• "This list is for those of us who obsess over every subject line, not because we have to—but because we care."

The result? Readers started using her language in replies. The words created community without requiring structure.

Inviting Participation Without Losing Control

Jenna didn't want to run a forum. She didn't want to moderate threads or answer questions all day.

But she *did* want her readers to shape the experience.

So she began asking small things:

- "What would make this series better?"

- "Want to see a teardown next week? Vote yes or no."

- "Reply with a tactic that worked for you—I might include it."

And when people responded, she included them. Quoted them. Credited them.

This wasn't crowdsourcing. It was co-creation.

Over time, readers began to expect this dynamic. They didn't just read Jenna's list. They influenced it.

That buy-in drove retention more than any automation ever could.

Creating Shared Rituals

One of Jenna's favorite moves was to create small traditions.

Every December, she sent "The Subject Line Awards," a roundup of the best headers from her list and others.

Each May, she did "Inbox Spring Cleaning," where she helped readers audit their own email habits.

These weren't content pieces. They were rituals.

And readers looked forward to them.

They forwarded them. They replied with their own entries. They posted screenshots on LinkedIn.

The list started to feel like a living thing—one with seasons, rhythms, memory.

That's what community is. Not just interaction, but shared time.

Giving the Readers a Voice

At first, Jenna feared asking too much. Would people care? Would they respond? Would it feel needy?

But when she tried asking open questions—"What's your biggest challenge with email right now?"—the replies flooded in.

She turned those replies into:

• Reader Q&A weeks

• Micro-case studies

• Free bonus guides

She let readers shape the content calendar.

This made the list more relevant. But more than that—it made it feel ours, not just hers.

Referability as a Signal of Belonging

Jenna noticed that readers forwarded her emails more often when she was vulnerable, not polished.

The best forwardable emails weren't the most "useful." They were the most *real*.

She started adding a simple line at the end:

"If this helped, send it to a friend who writes email and thinks too hard about commas."

That one sentence nearly doubled her organic growth rate.

Why? Because it wasn't about the list. It was about identity.

The reader wasn't just passing along content. They were saying, "This is who I am—and who I think you are too."

Communities grow through shared values. Not viral hooks.

Creating Quiet Spaces for Deeper Belonging

Jenna didn't want a Slack group. She didn't want a course

community.

So she created "Reply Circles."

Every quarter, she sent an invite:

"Want to join a 10-person email thread for two weeks? Just peers, no pitches. One prompt per week."

The result was extraordinary.

Readers formed real connections. Kept in touch. Some even started projects together.

Jenna wasn't the center of the circle. She was the *inviter*.

That act—of convening without controlling—made her list more than a list. It made her a connector.

Letting the Work Outlive the Writer

Community doesn't just live in live events or replies. It lives in impact.

Jenna started seeing her frameworks pop up in places she'd never sent them. A coaching program referenced her teardown method. A startup used her reengagement flow. A newsletter linked to her "No CTA Email."

At first, she bristled. It felt like loss of control.

But then she reframed it. This wasn't plagiarism. This was proliferation.

Her ideas were living beyond her. And in that way, her list became a cultural signal.

She started giving more things away. No gate. No opt-in. Just trust.

Because the more people carried her ideas, the more the community grew.

Even when she wasn't looking.

Creating Space for the Next Version of the Community

After five years of writing weekly, Jenna felt the edges of evolution.

Her tone wanted to shift. Her readers had matured. New people joined who hadn't seen the early days.

So she wrote a letter:

"This list is changing. Not going away. Just growing up."

She invited old readers to stay. New ones to help shape the next chapter.

She shared what might change:

• More strategy, less tactics

• Longer essays

• New voices and guest interviews

She gave her readers a say.
Not in whether it changed. But in how.
That's how you future-proof a community. You invite people into the future.

Why the List Lasted

When people ask Jenna why her list worked so long, she doesn't say "great subject lines" or "smart segmentation."

She says:

"Because I never forgot there were humans on the other side. And I let them in."

Her emails weren't content. They were conversation.
Her subscribers weren't leads. They were co-creators.
Her list wasn't an audience. It was a community.
Because she made it one.

Section Recap: From Broadcast to Belonging

A healthy email list grows stronger when:

- Readers see themselves in the message

- Identity replaces transaction

- Language creates shared space

- Engagement becomes contribution

- Leadership makes room for participation

In Chapter 10, we'll bring everything together. The final blueprint. Not a checklist, but a way of thinking.

Because if you want an email list that lasts, it has to be built not just on strategy—but on story.

Chapter 10

The Final Blueprint:

Designing a Practice That Lasts

Section 1: The Shift From Strategy

To Story

"Email is not going to disappear. Possibly ever. Until the robots kill us all."
— Paul Buchheit (Creator of Gmail)

For years, Jenna followed strategy. She studied it. She executed it. She tested it. Strategy was what she leaned on when the path ahead felt uncertain. It gave her direction, control, clarity. And it worked. Strategy brought growth. It gave her a voice in a crowded space. It turned ideas into revenue.

But at a certain point, she hit a ceiling.

Not a financial one. Not even a creative one. She hit a ceiling of *resonance*. Her emails were still good. The metrics were solid. She was publishing on time, engaging readers, selling products. But she could feel something was missing. The energy had changed. The spark had dulled.

She realized she was no longer writing from story. She was writing from plan.

And while strategy can sustain a system, only story can sustain a soul.

This final chapter is about the return to story. Not as a format, but as a foundation. Because the most durable email lists—the ones that grow, resonate, and endure—aren't built on tactics alone. They're built on a worldview. A narrative. A purpose.

Jenna didn't abandon strategy. She integrated it into something deeper. A way of seeing. A way of serving. A way of being in someone's inbox—not just as a sender, but as a signal.

The Difference Between a Tactic and a Story

A tactic is what you do. A story is what you believe.

Jenna's early emails worked not because they followed best practices, but because they were anchored in a point of view. She believed email was a conversation, not a campaign. She believed subject lines weren't clickbait—they were trust tests. She believed replies mattered more than clicks.

And that belief gave her a center.

When she forgot that—when she got caught in the whirlwind of growth hacking and segmentation and optimization—her list didn't crash. But it drifted.

Drift isn't loud. It's subtle. But over time, it shows up.

• You hesitate before writing.

• You write more about what will work than what you care about.

• Your best lines feel technical, not true.

Jenna began her return to story with a question:

"What do I still believe about this work?"

She wrote it out.

• I believe inboxes are sacred.

• I believe email is the most intimate digital space.

• I believe the best marketing doesn't feel like marketing.

That exercise didn't produce a strategy. It produced *alignment*.
And alignment became momentum.

Story as the Engine of Email

Once she returned to her core beliefs, everything else clarified.

Subject lines stopped being puzzles. They became invitations. Open rates stopped being metrics. They became signals. Content stopped being deliverables. It became dialogue.

Every tactic still mattered. But each now lived inside a larger narrative.

Jenna saw that the emails that performed best—the ones that built community, sold out workshops, got shared in Slack channels—had one thing in common: they reinforced the story her readers told about themselves.

She wasn't just writing to her readers. She was writing *with* them.

And that's when email became sustainable again. Not because she had a new funnel. But because she had a renewed frame.

Rewriting the Role of the Email Marketer

In most circles, the email marketer is a tactician. They optimize flows. Split-test headers. Watch heatmaps.

But Jenna redefined the role for herself. She was a narrator. A connector. A guide.

Her job wasn't to fill the calendar. It was to craft a journey.

She stopped asking:

- What should I send next week?

- What product should I promote this quarter?

- What's the next growth lever?

She started asking:

- What chapter are my readers in?

- What question are they sitting with?

- What conversation wants to continue?

Those shifts rewired her practice.

She wasn't just running a content engine. She was hosting a long, ongoing, permission-based story.

Your List as a Living Book

Jenna began to treat her list like a serialized memoir.

Each email was a page. Each series was a chapter. Each year was a volume.

This mindset gave her space. Permission. Depth.

She didn't need to summarize everything in one email. She could unfold ideas slowly. She didn't need to be universally valuable every time. She could stay in theme, let tension build. She didn't need to shout. Because readers who follow stories *lean in*.

The result? Her writing got better. Her tone got braver. Her subscribers stayed longer.

Because when a reader enters a story, they don't just consume. They *commit*.

Building Email Around Transformation

Every story is about change. And Jenna realized her most resonant emails weren't the ones that taught something. They were the ones that moved someone.

From confusion to clarity. From doubt to action. From silence to reply.

She started mapping her content around transformation—not information.

What does my reader believe now? What do I want them to believe after this email?

Those questions helped her shape narrative arcs across weeks, not just messages.

She layered depth. She returned to key themes. She echoed earlier ideas in new ways.

Readers noticed. They said:

- "This feels like a journey."

- "It's like you're in my head."

- "Each email builds on the last."

That's not automation. That's authorship.

Letting the Reader Be the Hero

In most email marketing, the sender is the expert. The list is the audience.

But Jenna knew from storytelling that every great narrative puts the *reader* at the center.

She wasn't Gandalf. She was the map.

Her job wasn't to be the voice of authority. It was to help her reader feel their own agency, clarity, power.

She wrote emails that said:

"You already know more than you think." "You've done harder things than this." "What would it look like to trust your voice this week?"

And readers responded. Not because they were impressed. But because they were invited.

Why Story Lasts and Strategy Shifts

Platforms change. Tools evolve. Algorithms break.

But stories endure.

The story Jenna told—about intimacy in the inbox, about human-centered email, about voice as the real deliverability trick—didn't need updates.

It evolved with her. It grew with her readers. But it stayed rooted.

And when tactics stopped working, the story still held.

She wasn't starting over. She was continuing.

That's what made her list sustainable.

Not just relevant. *Resilient.*

How to Find Your Story

Jenna didn't have a brand book or manifesto. She had a set of personal truths.

She wrote them every year. Not to market. To remember.

• What do I believe about attention?

• What do I want to protect in this work?

• What do I wish more marketers would say out loud?

These became her filters. If a strategy contradicted her answers, she didn't use it.

If a reader aligned with her truths, she welcomed them.

That's how she grew a list that resonated. By writing from belief—not just technique.

Story as the Simplifier

When Jenna hit overwhelm—too many ideas, too many offers, too many metrics—she came back to story.

"What's the story I want to tell this month?"

That one question cut through the noise.

It shaped what to write. What to sell. What to hold.

Story wasn't just her voice. It was her editor.

When the Story Changes

One year, Jenna noticed she felt restless. Her usual themes felt distant. Her reader's questions had changed.

So she gave herself permission to shift.

She wrote to her list:

"The story I've been telling is changing. And if you're in that same season, I hope you'll stay."

241

Some readers left. The right ones stayed. New ones arrived.

Because a true list doesn't follow content. It follows story. And a true story has chapters.

Jenna began a new one.

With the same voice. The same truth. The same belief:

That an email list isn't a number. It's a narrative.

And when you build from that place—you don't just grow. You last.

Section Recap: The Center That Holds

Tactics change. Trends fade. But a story—anchored in belief, built on trust, shaped around transformation—can guide your practice for years.

In Section 2, we'll walk through Jenna's final integration—how she blended story and strategy into a living system. One that adapts, delivers, sells, and connects. Not from pressure. But from purpose.

Chapter 10 - Section 2

Integrating the Moving Parts
A Living Email System

By the time Jenna had written hundreds of emails, launched a handful of products, and turned a simple subscriber list into a thriving community, she knew what worked. Not just once, or for a single campaign, but over years.

But what made her practice last wasn't a single template, framework, or tactic. It was the integration of everything she had learned into a *living system*—a flexible, responsive structure built on trust, rhythm, and resonance.

This system wasn't a machine. It was more like a garden. It needed tending, yes—but it also adapted to seasons. It didn't require force. It required attention.

In this section, we explore how Jenna put the pieces together. Not as a rigid plan, but as an evolving practice.

Because if you want your list to thrive—not just survive—you have to think like a builder, feel like a host, and act like a steward.

A Calendar That Breathes

Jenna no longer followed a content calendar in the traditional sense. What she built instead was a rhythm map.

Each month had a natural arc:

- The first week set the tone—story, insight, or reflection

- The middle weeks delivered teaching, examples, or responses

- The final week invited—an offer, a question, a next step

This gave her structure without suffocation.

When a new idea landed, she had space to insert it. When a product was ready, she didn't need to build urgency—it fit.

She gave herself one wild card per month: an email she could write off-theme, off-script, entirely from intuition. These became reader favorites.

That freedom kept her writing sharp.

Offer Design That Mirrors the Narrative

Each offer Jenna created came from inside the story she was already telling.

She never launched a course just because it was Q2. She launched a course because readers were replying with the same question, the same confusion, the same hunger.

She didn't have a product funnel. She had a product path.

One offer helped readers gain confidence. The next helped them deepen skill. Another supported scaling.

And all of them reflected the same values:

• Respect for the reader's time

• Clear articulation of outcomes

• Design built around action, not overwhelm

She viewed every product as a chapter. Not a sale, but a stage.
This made her sales feel like progression, not pressure.

Subscriber Onboarding That Begins With Belief

Instead of dropping new subscribers into a content treadmill, Jenna welcomed them like a guest.

Her onboarding sequence began with story—hers and theirs.

The first email shared why she writes, and what kind of relationship she hopes to have. The second introduced her favorite idea. The third asked what brought them here. The fourth invited them to co-create.

These weren't preambles. They were positioning.

By the time a subscriber finished that sequence, they didn't just know what Jenna did. They knew *who she was*.

And that shifted everything.

New readers opened more, replied more, bought more—not because of clever segmentation, but because of aligned expectation.

Retention Systems That Feel Like Rituals

Jenna stopped looking at retention as a performance metric. She saw it as a sign of emotional continuity.

The goal wasn't to reduce churn. The goal was to continue the relationship.

She designed simple touchpoints:

• A quarterly best-of recap that resurfaced her most resonant ideas

• A "Just checking in" email sent to dormant subscribers, with no pitch—just a pulse

• A yearly thank-you letter to long-time readers

She automated where it made sense. But the tone was always personal.

When readers felt remembered, they stayed.

Not because they were hooked. Because they felt held.

Growth That Reflects the Reader's Journey

For years, Jenna chased growth. Later, she let it come to her.

She aligned every growth strategy with the story her list was telling:

• Podcast appearances that matched her tone

• Guest writing that extended her narrative

• Partnerships with people her readers already trusted

She never bought leads. She never ran cold ads.

She asked: "Will the person this attracts feel at home in the inbox I've built?"

If the answer was yes, she greenlit the campaign. If not, she passed—even if the numbers were tempting.

Her subscriber count didn't skyrocket. But her reply rates doubled. Her sales increased. Her churn slowed.

Because readers weren't traffic. They were characters in the story.

A Personal Practice Around the List

Jenna didn't just *manage* her list. She maintained a relationship *with it*.

She built rituals not just for writing, but for reflecting.

Every Monday, she read replies. Every Friday, she reviewed engagement. Once a month, she wrote one email just for herself—no send, no polish, just truth.

She used that time to ask:

• What feels exciting?

• What feels stale?

• What am I trying to say but not saying?

That self-awareness translated to stronger writing. Not because she was clearer on message. Because she was closer to herself.

Letting the System Evolve

Over time, the system changed.

Her calendar shifted. Her offers changed formats. Her list segmentation simplified.

But the principles stayed the same:

- Write like a human.

- Invite, don't push.

- Build for the season, not the algorithm.

The system didn't require Jenna to always be "on." It supported her when she needed rest.

And when she returned, it welcomed her back.

Why This Works (Even When You're Tired)

Any system can function in peak performance seasons.

But Jenna's system worked in the messy ones too. When she felt lost. When she doubted herself. When life pulled her attention away.

Because she didn't build it for performance. She built it for *resilience*.

A structure designed to hold, not hustle.

This allowed her to write not just when it was easy, but when it mattered.

And that's why her list lasted.

Because it was never about the next send. It was about the *relationship over time*.

The Living System at a Glance

Jenna's email practice wasn't a funnel. It was a field.

She planted seeds (ideas). Watered them (conversations). Pruned when needed (list clean-up). Harvested at the right time (offers).

Each part connected to the others. Nothing stood alone.
And most importantly—it all reflected who she was.
That integration created integrity.
And readers feel integrity. They trust it. They stay for it.

Section Recap: Build Something That Lives

This section brought Jenna's entire system into view:

- A rhythm map instead of a rigid calendar

- Offer arcs that reflect reader transformation

- Onboarding built around belief

- Retention as recognition, not just performance

- Growth tied to values, not volume

- A personal practice for reflection and return

In the final section of this book, we'll close with Jenna's parting message—what she tells every creator, writer, and marketer just starting out:

You don't need the perfect system. You need a system that lets you keep going. And the best ones? They're built from the inside out.

Chapter 10 - Section 3

The Final Note — You're Not Behind, You're Becoming

I f there was one sentence Jenna repeated more than any other to herself and to her students, it was this: "You're not behind. You're just becoming." It sounds simple. Maybe even a little soft. But it was the truth that steadied her—especially in seasons where everything felt scattered, delayed, uncertain, or less-than.

Because the world of email—of marketing, business, online growth—constantly tells you that you're falling behind. Behind in growth. Behind in tech. Behind in tactics. That everyone else is executing better, faster, louder.

But the truth is that the only sustainable email list is the one that grows *with* you. Not as a monument to some past version of your voice. Not as a machine that must be fed daily. But as a living record of your evolution.

This final section is not a summary of tactics. It's an affirmation of identity. Because after a decade of building an email practice that truly lasted, Jenna understood something most people miss:

The most powerful email list isn't the one with the most subscribers. It's the one that reflects the *realest* version of the person writing it.

Becoming a Voice, Not a Brand

When Jenna first started, she thought she needed to be a brand. She created a logo. Picked fonts. Drafted a mission statement that sounded like every other mission statement. And for a while, it gave her confidence.

But over time, she realized that her readers didn't come for the polish. They came for the voice.

Not just the tone. Not just the phrasing. But the sense of *presence* behind every word.

Voice is what makes a list durable. When a reader hears something in their head that sounds like you, *you've arrived.*

So she stopped optimizing for branding. And started optimizing for *recognition.*

Could a reader tell, in the first sentence, that this was Jenna? That became her bar.

Not slick. Not perfect. Just unmistakably hers.

You Don't Need to Scale to Matter

Some of Jenna's peers scaled. Big lists. Big teams. Big launches.

She cheered them on. But she chose a different path.

She kept her operation lean. She stayed close to the writing. She made space for seasons of quiet.

And because of that, her readers felt safe with her. Safe to unsubscribe and return. Safe to not buy, then buy later. Safe to say, "This one didn't land," and know they'd still be welcome.

Jenna called it the slow email movement. Not in pace. But in depth.

She didn't scale by force. She scaled by *layer*. Each email adding richness, history, relationship.

And that mattered more than any growth chart.

There Will Be Gaps

Jenna wanted every chapter to flow. Every series to arc. Every product to land with precision.

But real life isn't tidy.

She missed sends. She changed offers mid-launch. She disappeared for a month once.

And still—her list held.

Not because she never faltered. But because she had built enough trust that when she said, "I'm back," her readers believed her.

Consistency is not perfection. It's return.

That was the real lesson. You don't need to never mess up. You just need to come back honestly.

You Will Outgrow Your Frameworks

There was a point when Jenna's favorite email structure stopped working. Not because the framework was flawed. But because she had changed.

Her voice had matured. Her ideas had deepened. Her readers had grown with her.

She didn't scrap everything. She adapted.

She let go of three-step intros. She experimented with longform stories. She paused sequences that once felt sacred.

She stopped asking, "What's worked before?" And started asking, "What wants to be said now?"

That shift made space for something bigger: Not a new tactic. A truer voice.

Your List Is a Legacy, Not a List

Jenna didn't start writing email to build a legacy. But years in, she could see it clearly.

The thousands of words sent. The relationships formed. The quiet influence on teams and writers and marketers who never even replied—but always read.

This was her body of work. Not her content. Her *conversation*.

And that conversation was a thread. A breadcrumb trail. Something future readers could follow.

She kept every email. Every version. Every draft.

Not to reuse. To remember.

Because in a world that deletes, archives, and forgets—email is one of the few places where your voice *stays*.

That's the legacy.

Not reach. Resonance.

When You Feel Like Quitting

Everyone does. Jenna did, too.

The unsubscribe waves. The low-reply streaks. The launches that didn't land.

John Elder

She had drafts she never sent. Ideas that never made it past the outline. Seasons where she wondered if anyone cared anymore.

But then—always—a reply. A line like:

"I've been reading for years. I've never replied until now. But today's note changed everything."

And in that moment, the noise fell away.

Because it was never about volume. It was about *that*. That one reader. That one change. That moment of recognition between one human and another.

That's the heart of email.

Not automation. Not monetization. Not even communication.

But recognition.

If You're Just Starting Out

Jenna's advice was always the same. Start small. Write what's true. Let your voice find you.

You don't need a framework. You need a reason.

A reason to show up. A reason to write. A reason to care.

And if you do it well, readers will find you. They'll tell you who they are. They'll show you what they need.

And if you listen carefully enough, they'll shape your best work.

Email isn't a platform. It's a mirror.

It reflects who you are. And helps you see the people who want to walk with you.

That's the work. That's the path.

That's the blueprint.

Not a tactic. Not a system. But a *practice*.

One built from the inside out.

One that never stops becoming.

The Final Line

Jenna still sends emails. Not because she has to. Because she *gets to*.

Because somewhere out there, someone is opening one of her notes. Reading slowly. Smiling. Forwarding it to a friend.

And thinking:

"This is exactly what I needed today."

That is the kind of email list that lasts.
Not because it was built to scale. But because it was built to *matter*.

John Elder

Appendix

Where To Go From Here?

If you enjoyed this book and want to continue the conversation, please subscribe to my email newsletter and podcast; "Spamnesty" over at **Spamnesty.com** where I discuss all things email marketing. I've also got a new book coming out soon called "Spam Dunk: Taking Your Emails from Spambox to Inbox". If it's not out yet, subscribing to my newsletter or listening to my podcast is the best way to hear about it!

You can also follow me at **JohnElder.com** where you can find links to all my social media stuff and things.

John Elder

About The Author

John Elder is one of the original founders of Internet Marketing. He created one of the Internet's earliest advertising networks (BannerClicks.com) in 1997 and sold it to publicly traded WebQuest International, Inc. (WEBQ) at the height of the first dot com boom. He then built a biotech b2b company (VitalBio.com) and sold it to a group of investment bankers. After that he developed the award-winning Submission-Spider search engine submission software that was used by over 10% of active internet users at the time. He then built a network of over 4,000 affiliate websites selling millions of products, in what became an eerily similar precursor to Google Shopping.

John then founded **Codemy.com,** an online school where he's taught over 20 million people to code. He has created over 100 online coding courses in Python, Ruby, Javascript, Tkinter, Django, Rails, PHP, HTML, CSS, MySQL, PostGres, SQL, PyGame, Kivy, PyQT, and more. He's also written several best-selling coding books.

Today he teaches email marketing through his podcast and newsletter at **Spamnesty.com.**

John graduated with honors from Washington University in St. Louis and lives with his wife April in Las Vegas with their dogs Aspen and Ivy.

Disclaimer

The strategies, tactics, and examples in this book are provided solely for educational and informational purposes. Nothing herein should be construed as legal, financial, accounting, or other professional advice, and no warranty, express or implied, is made regarding the revenue, profit, or other results you may achieve by applying any concepts discussed. Business outcomes depend on numerous factors—including individual skill, market conditions, and execution—and therefore cannot be guaranteed. You alone are responsible for your actions and their consequences; before implementing any recommendations, you should perform your own due diligence and, where appropriate, consult qualified professionals. The author and publisher expressly disclaim all liability for any loss or damages, direct or consequential, that may result from the use of the material contained in this book.

www.ingramcontent.com/pod-product-compliance
Lightning Source LLC
Chambersburg PA
CBHW031403180326
41458CB00043B/6598/J